IN THE AFTERMATH
OF THE STORM

IN THE AFTERMATH OF THE STORM

Stories of Hope and Healing

Edited by:
Jennifer N. Fenwick

Jennifer N. Fenwick
Visit my website at https://moth-journal.com/
on Facebook @MothJournal
or on Instagram @mothjournal14

Printed in the United States of America

First Printing: October 2019
Amazon Kindle Direct Publishing

ISBN-9781692986902

DEDICATION

For those who survived. Those who reached out to help in those first hours, days and weeks. Those who selflessly continued to give as the months passed. Those who rose up. Those who continue to rise. Those who suffered then; who continue to suffer now. For souls everywhere who know what it's like to survive a disaster of this magnitude. Who, even in the face of heart-breaking odds, never give up. This is for you.

CONTENTS

Jennifer N. Fenwick

ACKNOWLEDGEMENTS

In the Aftermath of the Storm: Stories of Hope and Healing is the sequel to *In the Eye of the Storm: Stories of Survival and Hope from the Florida Panhandle*, which debuted in January 2019, just three months after Hurricane Michael slammed into the Florida Panhandle.

In the Eye of the Storm told the stories of the survivors; in their own words and pictures; in their poetry and art. All proceeds from book sales both online and through local merchants benefit the *Hurricane Michael Relief Fund* through the *United Way of Northwest Florida* (UWNWFL). One-hundred percent of donations to this fund remain in the Panhandle assisting those most in need.

The contributors and I are grateful to our sponsors, whose generous donations allowed us to provide books for local distribution.

This past year has brought many changes to our lives and homes. While some areas are showing signs of recovery and rebuilding, other areas look just as they did the morning after the storm.

None of us who survived that day emerged unchanged. Whether it was the destruction all around us or the grief we carried in our hearts, October 10, 2018 will forever mark a defining moment in our lives.

In the Aftermath of the Storm continues our story. It's been a year of tears and grief, a year of frustration and disappointment, a year of hope and healing. The road ahead is long, but by the grace of God and the strength of our faith and conviction, we will go on. We will continue rebuilding. We will continue moving forward. But we will never forget.

Like its predecessor, the stories, poetry, and images contained in this book come from the many residents who survived Hurricane Michael and who continue to work tirelessly to rebuild their lives and livelihoods. I am grateful for their willingness to share their stories and art with me.

Linda Artman
Amy Boe
Thomas Cook ⎽5 6, 82
Jason Davis
Andrea Boulette Dow
John Fenwick
Erica McNabb Floyd
Melinda JD Hall
Jason Hedden
Elise Henkel
Kim Mixon Hill
Richard Hill
Deborah Hinton
Teri Elizabeth Hord
Tracy Johnstone
Karsun Designs Photography
Sandi Klug-Lard
Cynthia McCauley
Laura McManus
Tony Miller
Lisa Munson
Shaun Mulligan
Sharon Owens
Heather Parker
Jan Prewett
Jane Smith

◆ ◆ ◆

AUTHOR'S NOTE

Hurricane Michael made landfall in the early afternoon hours of October 10, 2018, in the Florida Panhandle. With maximum sustained winds of 161 mph, Michael's eye came ashore near the tiny coastal community of Mexico Beach, FL.

When we emerged from the shelters we had hurriedly taken, we were greeted with an eerie silence. The world we knew was gone and we were left instead with nothing but overpowering shock and grief.

Over the course of the next days, weeks, and months, stories began to emerge. Stories that broke our hearts while at the same time, inspiring and strengthening our resolve and determination. There are so many stories. As Tony Simmons, a writer for the *News Herald* wrote a few weeks after the storm, "We all became storytellers that day."

In the Aftermath of the Storm: Stories of Hope and Healing, is the sequel to *In the Eye of the Storm*, which released in January 2019. Like our first book, which focused on survival, *In the Aftermath of the Storm* is a collection of stories, poetry, and images created as we've moved through the phases of recovery.

From heartbreak and grief to hope and rebuilding, these are our words. Each story, poem, and image included comes from the heart of the people who survived and who are continuing to live in the aftermath.

Like its predecessor, all proceeds from book sales go directly to the *Hurricane Michael Relief Fund* to help those struggling in the aftermath and to assist with rebuilding communities and lives. #850strong

Jennifer N. Fenwick

There are no greater treasures than the highest human qualities such as compassion, courage, and hope. Not even tragic accident or disaster can destroy such treasures of the heart.

— *DAISAKU IKEDA*

IN THE AFTERMATH

In the aftermath we said goodbye
To so many things.
The trees.
Our homes.
Our landmarks.
Our cities.
We grieved our losses.
For ourselves.
For each other.
For our shattered lives.
We promised to rebuild.
To have faith.
To believe.
To hope.
But the goodbyes?
The goodbyes would remain.
How could they not?
When everywhere we looked,
Reminders.
Brokenness.
Heartbreak.
The goodbyes changed us forever.
In the aftermath we cried.
We prayed.
We struggled.
We yearned.
For the day we could breathe again.
For the moment we'd finally begin to heal.

—Jennifer N. Fenwick, March 24, 2019

Time seemed to stop that day, and is now marked forever as life before and after Hurricane Michael. Photo by Jan Prewett

What matters most is how well you walk through the fire."

— *CHARLES BUKOWSKI*

CAT 5: WHAT IT'S LIKE TO LIVE IN THE AFTERMATH

by Jennifer N. Fenwick

May 15, 2019—There have only been four. Only four recorded Atlantic storms have maintained category five strength as they barreled inland. The Labor Day Hurricane of 1935, with its maximum sustained winds of 185 mph, was the most intense to ever make landfall. It destroyed nearly all structures in the upper Florida Keys as it came ashore on the evening of September 3, 1935.

Hurricane Camille is the second-strongest hurricane to make landfall in the United States. Coming ashore just before midnight on August 17, 1969 along the Mississippi Gulf Coast with maximum sustained winds of 175 mph, Camille tore a path of total and utter destruction through the region, killing over 140 people with its extremely high storm surge and massive flooding. It was decades before the region fully recovered from the devastation.

Hurricane Andrew made landfall around Ellicott Key, Florida on August 24, 1992 with maximum sustained winds of 165 mph, making it the third strongest category five storm on record to hit the U.S. Andrew produced devastating damage across southern sections of Miami and nearly completely wiped Homestead, FL off the map. The damage total in Florida alone after Andrew was over $26 billion.

The most recent category 5 hurricane to devastate the Gulf Coast was Hurricane Michael, who made landfall in the early afternoon hours of October 10, 2018 along the Panhandle of Florida. With maximum sustained winds of 161 mph, Michael's eye came ashore near the tiny coastal community of Mexico Beach, FL. With its minimum central pressure of 27.13 inches, Michael also holds the distinction of being the third-most intense U. S. storm ever (behind Katrina, 2005, and Andrew, 1992).

Hurricane Michael caused catastrophic damage from winds and storm surge in the Panama City, Mexico Beach, and Cape San Blas areas. Michael was directly responsible for at least 79 deaths, including 59 in the U.S. and 15 in Central America and over $53 billion in damage, including $5 billion in property damage in Florida alone and almost $4 billion to Florida's forestry and farming communities.

Keep your head up Panama City. A feat that has proven much harder as the weeks since Michael have turned into months. Photo by Sharon Owens

An Eerie Silence. In the early afternoon hours of October 10, 2018, Hurricane Michael barreled into the Florida Panhandle altering our lives in ways we could never have imagined or prepared for. When we emerged from the shelters we had hurriedly taken, we were greeted with an eerie silence.

Over the course of the next few days, weeks, and months, stories began to emerge. Stories that broke our hearts while at the same time, inspiring and strengthening our resolve and determination to overcome the chaos all around us.

There were so many stories. Like the emergency responder who dropped everything immediately after the winds died down, leaving his home to travel to the very center of the destruction in Mexico Beach only to return to his home days later to find that everything of value he'd left behind had been taken by looters.

The story of the young couple who sheltered in a three-story bank building near their townhome, only to be forced into a stairwell as the windows blew out all around them. Their saving grace was the dog leash they'd secured around the stairwell door to protect their pets. As the intense fury of Michael's winds swept through the building, that leash kept the doors from blowing open, sparing their lives as well.

The story of the father and son who exchanged "I love you's" during the height of the storm, fearing death was imminent as trees fell on their home and they wrestled valiantly to keep the doors closed against the wind while Mom used every pot and bucket available to keep the rain from flooding the interior. Or the story of the new parents forced to sleep in their car with their newborn infant after their home was totally destroyed and they had nowhere else to go.

A Mexico Beach resident, Scott Boutell, was close to tears as he spoke to a reporter in front of his wrecked house a few days after the storm: "Our lives are gone here. All the stores, all the restaurants, everything. There's nothing left here anymore," he said (Richard Luscombe, *The Guardian*, 11 OCT 2018).

Only the basics remained. As the days and weeks began to blur and muddy, we were stripped to the very basics of survival. No power, phones, or internet meant no communication with the world outside. And no way for family members outside the Panhandle to know for certain if their loved ones were still among the living.

No grocery stores, gas stations or drinkable water, meant we had to rely on the kindness of strangers and volunteers for our basic needs. Entire neighborhoods banded together to pool available resources and in some cases, to provide shelter for those who lost everything.

The arduous task of digging ourselves out of the destruction, literally, began as soon as equipment could be obtained. Rescue teams went door-to-door, combing through wreckage to check for survivors, helping to dig out those trapped, or to remove the deceased who had not been so lucky.

Large red X's began to appear on doors across the region, a way of marking that the dwelling had been checked and cleared. It was like moving through the set of one of those apocalyptic movies, only the set was real, and we were the bedraggled cast of shell-shocked, weary survivors. **And the eerie quiet remained pervasive.**

In the immediate aftermath, 4,000 National Guard were deployed to assist the nearly 2,000 law-enforcement officials already on the ground in the area. Crews with dogs searched door-to-door in Mexico Beach, pushing aside debris to get inside badly damage structures (Richard Luscombe, *The Guardian*, 11 OCT 2018).

A strictly enforced dawn to dusk curfew was put in place to protect us, but also to deter looters from taking advantage of the plight of others.

Within a day, over 6,000 linemen descended on the area to get the decimated power-grid back online as quickly as possible. It wouldn't be quick. It would take over a month to restore the nearly one million homes and businesses affected throughout the region.

Work crews removed 31 million cubic yards of debris in Florida, compared to 3 million for Hurricane Irma, a much broader storm that affected the entire peninsula in 2017, according to T.J. Dargan, deputy federal coordinating officer for the Federal Emergency Management Agency's Hurricane Michael response and recovery effort (Patricia Sullivan and Joel Achenbach, *The Washington Post*, 6 APR 2019).

However, the aftermath still continues unabated. Our homeless numbers are on the rise. Livable properties are scarce, and supply and demand has caused rent prices to skyrocket. Bay County Schools reports some 4,800 students, about 1 in 6, are living in temporary homes, a classification federal officials consider as homeless.

A day-to-day struggle. Many of the lingering effects of the storm are more intangible. We are visibly fatigued, with stress, anxiety, and depression affecting us more and more. The constant and ever-present reminders of the storm are a blow to our psyche and a punch to the gut every single day.

During all this time, while we've been focused on survival, recovery, and healing, doing all we can to stand on our own, we *never* anticipated that some of our greatest frustrations and heartache would come at the hands of those we believed we could rely on most to assist us.

That the world quickly moved on and donations for Hurricane Michael relief have fallen well-short of those for previous storms and disasters hurt, yes, but we could understand that. We knew from the beginning that we were not the only natural disaster affecting the country. Other regions, most notably the victims of the wildfires that burned though California, and more recently, the victims of Hurricane Dorian, are also in need of assistance.

No. What sickened us most as the weeks turn into months, was the partisan politics in Washington that hampered the passage of the relief bill we so desperately needed. As lawmakers continued to spar over the details of the supplemental disaster funding bill, we, and all the other disaster affected regions in the country continued to suffer.

"If this hurricane had gone through Central Florida, South Florida, the dollars would have been there by now," said state Agricultural Commissioner Nicole "Nikki" Fried. "People are out there struggling every day — people whose entire life savings, entire college fund, is basically lying on the ground," (Patricia Sullivan and Joel Achenbach, *The Washington Post*, 6 APR 2019).

There are still trees resting on structures. There are still blue tarps covering damaged roofs. There are still pieces of plywood covering windows. There are still piles of rubble in parking lots and in neighborhoods where structures once stood. People are still living in tents. Others have lost all hope and are leaving the area for good.

Abandoned homes and structures are rampant throughout the region. In some areas progress is being made, in others, it looks much like it did the day after the storm. Photo by Jason Davis

Every day you hear stories of shady contractors taking advantage of desperate, weary people. Of battles with insurance companies leaving victims with scant resources to make much-needed repairs to homes and businesses. You wonder what it's like to live in the aftermath of a category 5 hurricane?

It's hell. We are doing our best, but it's a day-to-day struggle. In truth, we are still living in a war zone.

◆ ◆ ◆

HOW

How can we nurture,

when our world is broken?

How can we heal, when every day a new scar

is revealed? Is it wrong to feel defeated?

To want to sink beneath this overwhelming shattering.

To want to breathe, just once, without this sharp, stinging pain.

How can we move forward, when every moment is a reminder?

Of all we lost. Of all we'll never be again.

We survived the storm. But it was in the silent aftermath

that we finally understood. We'll never be the same.

—Jennifer N. Fenwick, March 12, 2019

Broken. Photo by Jan Prewett

SIX MONTHS

6 months post hurricane Michael.

How am I you ask?

Are things getting back to normal?

 I'll tell you how I am.

The outside of my house is looking much better.

 I have a new roof; I have new windows in progress.

I even have beautiful new colorful flowers outside my house.

But the inside looks a mess.

Like a family's merely surviving one day at a time.

Like we forgot what it was like to clean and organize

because we just don't have energy for that anymore.

Laundry in baskets, stacks of Hurricane paperwork lying about.

Dishevelled to say the least.

But you'd never know it from the outside of the house.

We have our fences mostly up

and it almost looks like we have our lives together.

This is the most accurate depiction of how I am doing.

On the outside I look like I'm doing ok,

 but inside I'm dishevelled and unorganized,

nervous and merely surviving one day at a time.

I have to perform as an actor at my newly acquired

post—hurricane job so the customers think

I'm a happy ball of joy.

Because nobody likes a sally sad sack.

This is daunting; so when I'm home I sleep.

Went out of town for the weekend

for my daughters state competition

and for a much-needed break from our new normal.

And when re-entering our broken area

that sadness came rushing back.

My new normal set it.

So how am I 6 months later?

I look like I have my act together.

Just don't knock and try to come inside.

—*Erica McNabb Floyd, April 10, 2019*

39 WEEKS

9 months today
39 weeks
Michael's children almost due
More than 39 weeps
More than 39 leaks
We're expecting a rain event today
Depression is topical
Call it tropical or storm
Both have the P, the T, the S and the D
Maybe we're just recycling those tears
Consuming our own
Don't sleep where you
Sit
Down
And tell me how is your fam?
Less blues on the rooves
But
His tarp is a sieve
Her attic's in view
Rents higher than spring breakers '02
Stop counting the days
Start clearing the haze
Why do I know it was a Wednesday?

—*Jason Hedden, July 11, 2019*

Photo by Jason Hedden

LET US NOT FORGET

Let us not forget;

Hurricane Michael was not just a storm,

It was a war.

A war we are still fighting.

Your love surrounded us then.

It surrounds us now.

Dear God, we believe Your promises.

You will restore all that is lost!

— Laura McManus, LCSW, August 6, 2019

A lone cross carved from the remains of a tree is the only sign of hope in the battered Sandy Creek region of the Florida Panhandle. Photo by Laura McManus

SUMMER SHOWERS

by Sandi Klug-Lard

"I found a massive dead rat in the shed," my husband said by way of greeting. Jesse stood in the doorway leading to our backyard, his black hair wet with humidity and sweat.

"That's disgusting." I crinkled my nose.

"Come look at it." He gestured behind him.

"Absolutely not!"

"Please!"

"No!" I stood up from my work at the table and walked to the kitchen. "Remember when you worked at the Mill and you sent me a text of that mouse caught in the trap! I'm scarred for life!"

"Yeah." Jesse laughed. "That was before trigger warnings. Well, come help me anyway. It's about to rain."

"No it isn't."

Jesse pulled on my arm and pointed to a dark cloud in the distance. Thunder rolled with emphasis. "Yes it is."

I went to put on my shoes while Jesse turned to finish his work outside. We had been working to clean out the shed, one of our last projects to complete since the hurricane happened nine months ago.

I walked out the back door and looked at the piles stretched out on the lawn.

"So what's the plan?" I asked Jesse.

He began counting on his fingers. "Trash is one pile. Keep. Sell."

We worked in silence for a while as the sky darkened around us.

"We should figure out how that rat got in," I said.

"I already looked. It shouldn't have been able to get in."

"Hmmmm," I pondered. "It must have happened when we left the door open for a bit after the storm, to let everything dry out."

The sky opened up then.

"Leave what's trash outside!" I yelled over the wind. "Sell pile to carport and Keep pile to shed!"

We hurried, but were soaked to the bone in less than a minute. Florida summer showers take no prisoners for the fifteen minutes they last.

I glanced over to my magnolia tree, a branch hung loose and swayed under the weight of the rain. It had split in half after the hurricane and my husband wanted to cut it down, but it was still growing. Maybe next summer I'd see my flowers again.

I noticed Jesse standing in the shed. He was no longer making an effort to be out in the rain helping me move items. Instead, he stood in the doorway while I handed him things to put away.

"I see you've given up!" I said teasingly.

"You know I don't like being rained on!"

A flash of memory, two teenagers playing in the rain.

"That's enough. Let's go inside!" Jesse yelled.

He set off at a fast pace through the grey mist while I trudged along, squinting towards the sky. My leggings stuck to my thighs like paste, my tank top hanging loosely around my shoulders. I raised my chin and put my arms out, catching the water before it hit the ground. I was a living fountain, every stream of water pouring off me in a steady flow.

Isn't it funny how people run from the rain, but pay to go to waterparks?

It's not that we don't like the rain, we just don't like the unexpected. We like to know when we're going to get wet, thank you very much. We like to pencil it into our schedules, not be surprised by it during chores or walking to our cars with bags of groceries. It's like paying money to watch a horror film. We like to be thrilled, but on our own terms with no real threat of danger.

I knew real fear. Being huddled in a small, stuffy room with a mattress pressed against a window. That was fear.

I knew storms, and this rain shower was no threat to me.

"What are you still doing out there?" My husband called from the door. He was standing in a new pair of boxers, his hair spiked up.

I walked over to the tree swing we put in for the kids. They lost their playhouse in the hurricane, so we installed the swing beneath our Pecan tree a few months later when we moved back in.

I positioned myself on the circular swing seat, the ropes digging into my skin.

"Come push me!' I shouted.

My husband hung his head, but I had no doubt that he would come to me. He put his head down and walked quickly through the sheets of water.

Standing beneath the leafy canopy, he gave me a push.

"Wheeee!!!!" And I laid back on the swing.

A memory. Two sleeping teenagers in a grey Kia.

"You remember our first date?" I said, the motion of the swing making me dreamily dizzy.

Jesse sighed. "Yes I do."

"Applebee's. I didn't want to go to work, so we went to the bridge after. It started to rain."

"I remember."

"I got out of the car to look out at the Bay. You hated it; I could tell."

"But I followed you."

"And you kissed me. Then we fell asleep in your Kia."

"I was not happy about you cutting work."

Photo by Sandi Klug-Lard

"I hated that job anyway." I smiled. "It was a good day."

The thunder rolled.

"Mom! Dad!" Our son called from the door. "What are you doing?"

"PLAYING!" I yelled back.

"You guys are weird." He shut the sliding glass door on our trip down memory lane.

"Can we go inside now?" My husband asked.

I put out my legs for him to catch, slowing me down. I stood up and looked at my husband. A little older. But not to me. To me, he was the guy who would always follow me into the rain, and tolerate it for my sake. And I kissed him, right there in the backyard of the home we made together. Soaking wet, cold and shivering.

Sixteen forever.

I could have sworn lightning shot through the sky then, a glow of energy that seemed to say—"We are here. We are here. We are here."

For a flash, a vapor of a moment, we're here. We live our lives, tell our stories and love our people well.

Like a Florida summer shower.

◆ ◆ ◆

CATEGORY 5

We didn't need the confirmation.
We already knew.
We felt the devastating winds.
Saw with our own eyes,
all the storm surge swept away.
We've lived in the aftermath.
Relentlessly. Since that day.
We've keenly felt the deaths.
The catastrophic devastation.
The destruction to our homes
and cities. Our livelihoods. Our spirit.
We understood, from the beginning.
the daunting task before us.
We cry for our children.
For the homeless.
For the beaten.
For the broken.
We help where we can.
Give what we can.
Comfort where we can.
Pray. Hope. We always will.
We didn't need confirmation.
From the beginning we understood.
This was always Category 5.
Maybe now, the world will understand.
And see us too.

—*Jennifer N. Fenwick, July 16, 2019*

HURRICANE MICHAEL: FIVE THINGS THE WORLD SHOULD KNOW

by Jennifer N. Fenwick

April 4, 2019—First, there was no way to adequately prepare. We'd done this before, many of us, more than once; prepared for the possibility of a hurricane visiting us during the Season. We were used to Summer ushering in, not just the tourists, but the Atlantic Hurricane Season as well. Hurricane Season begins the first of June and lasts through the end of November.

Living in the Panhandle of Florida, we knew that during any given Season we could be at risk, so preparedness was something we took seriously. Many of us had remained through Opal (1995) and Ivan (2004) and felt confident we could safely weather Michael as well.

But there are some things you can't prepare for. Some things that happen so quickly and change so dramatically that no amount of preparation matters. Hurricane Michael was one of those.

Hurricane Michael barreled into the Florida Panhandle during the early afternoon hours of October 10, 2018. Packing 161-mph sustained winds and a carrying a storm surge in excess of 16-ft, Michael wiped homes, businesses, structures, and acres upon acres of trees off the map.

"I think that if people are comparing storms, what was really fascinating was that Michael was still intensifying when it was making landfall," said AccuWeather Senior Meteorologist Dan Kottlowski, in an article that appeared in *Time Magazine*.

"Everyone has a story of loss they struggle to describe." *Photo by Jennifer Fenwick*

Second, the destruction was catastrophic and widespread. As the sun was beginning to set on the evening of October 10, residents in the path of Hurricane Michael emerged to a nightmare of unimaginable proportions.

"Nothing, and I stress NOTHING, could have prepared us for what we saw," said Jane Smith, who rode out the storm with her husband and son in their Bay County home. "I think at this point we went into shock." Smith and her family, like many, lost everything and are now trying to recover and rebuild in this new normal.

As the days crept by, the nightmare only worsened. Residents in the affected areas struggled to come to grips with the destruction of their homes and cities. Many who returned, once allowed, faced total destruction of their property. "Just 1 in 10 of Panama City's homes and businesses scraped by unscathed. The rest were damaged or destroyed, local officials said. The county property appraiser put the damage total in Bay County alone at $1.3 billion and counting," (Kathryn Varns, *Tampa Bay Times*, 27 DEC 2018).

Power was destroyed. Water was dangerous to use and consume. Cell and internet service was nonexistent. Cut off from the rest of the world, each day brought new struggles.

The impact from Michael is not just limited to the coastal region of the Florida Panhandle. The catastrophic damage spread well inland as Michael remained at hurricane strength into the rural and farming communities of Florida and southwest Georgia, before passing through Virginia and North Carolina, and then finally making his way back out to the Atlantic.

Three, the world moved on. We could not. Destroyed landmarks, street signs, and buildings made navigating the storm ravaged region tenuous at best. "People get lost driving around because landmarks were wiped out. They spray-paint their address on a piece of plywood and lean it against the garage door. They eat dinner in a McDonald's surrounded by construction workers chowing down on quarter-pounders," (*Tampa Bay Times*, 27 DEC 2018).

And while basic necessities have been restored, life here is far from normal as we continue to struggle.

Currently, some displaced families are living in a tent city in the backyard of one generous couple who decided that instead of turning their backs, they'd do something instead. Others have been forced to take shelter in campers, parked in the driveways of homes without roofs, sometimes without structures at all. Still others have been forced to return to their all-but-leveled apartment complexes because there is simply nowhere else to go.

To make matters worse, donations for Michael to three of the top disaster aid organizations have fallen well below the national average for similar storms, like Harvey, Florence, and Irma, who also hit the South in the past two years. "Survivors of Hurricane Michael fear that they've been forgotten," (*The Washington Post*, 6 APRIL 2019).

Four, the numbers don't lie. In Bay County alone, 5,500 students have had to leave their living situations because of hurricane damage (*News Herald*, 28 MAR 2019). Skyrocketing rent prices have further compounded the housing crisis (*My Panhandle*, 22 MAR 2019). Health officials report that signs of mental health problems and trauma are on the rise following Michael, including an increase in the number of Baker Act incidents in the school district (*WJHG*, 13 MAR 2019).

More than 3 million acres of Florida's forestry industry were severely damaged by Michael and about half of the damage was catastrophic, meaning 95 percent of the trees were lost, according to the Florida Forestry Service. With large tracts of managed land in the region, the storm is expected to cost the timber industry more than $1.3 billion (*News Herald*, updated 1 APR 2019).

In Florida, cotton farmers essentially lost most of the season's crop, which was ready for harvesting when it was swept away by the 161-mph winds. Aquaculture along the Gulf Coast, including oyster farming, suffered 80 to 100 percent losses from Michael (Jim Turner, *News Service of Florida*).

Michael barreled through Georgia at Cat 3 strength causing nearly $2.5 billion in damage, to the state's agricultural industry. State agriculture commissioner Gary Black said the losses were "our worst dreams being realized." Crops of all kinds—cotton, timber, and vegetables—suffered heavy damages. (*Atlanta Magazine*, 17 JAN 2019).

Hurricane Michael left nearly seven times the debris of Hurricane Irma, which barreled across 45 counties in 2017 (*Pensacola News Journal*, 8 JAN 2019).

Hurricane Michael is responsible for 35 deaths in Florida, 45 total (*NBC Miami*, 28 OCT 2018).

"Of all the Florida Panhandle areas affected by Michael, Bay County was hardest hit. Officials said almost three-quarters of its 68,000 households were affected. Former Florida House Speaker Allan Bense, who is leading a hurricane recovery initiative, estimated about 20,000 people were homeless in the weeks after the October storm," (Mike Schneider, *AP News*, 4 MAR 2019).

Fifth, the future may be uncertain, but we remain determined.

As we navigate this strange new world, there are days when the frustration and grief become overwhelming. Days when the determination grows stronger. Days when the fatigue and stress settle deeper into our bones.

Through it all, we try to remain hopeful. The world may have moved on, the impacts of Michael may still be revealing themselves, recovery and rebuilding may be ongoing with no definitive end in sight, but there's one thing we're all certain of, it will be a long time, and a lot of hard work, before we are OK again.

◆ ◆ ◆

Historic downtown Marianna, FL, like many locations throughout the region, was devastated by Michael. *Photo by Robert Blouin/Shutterstock*

WHAT CAN I DO?

by Sandi Klug-Lard

May 28, 2019—"So I hear things are still bad," they say.

"They are," I answer.

"What can I do? What organization can I donate to?"

It's well intentioned, from big hearted people. They know my town is still destroyed. They want to help.

So I send them to an organization and they probably give some of their hard earned money to it.

But I wish I could give them my real answer.

After Hurricane Michael hit, we received an influx of donations. Toys for kids, diapers, formula, bottled water—SO much bottled water—tarps, mattresses, food—nonperishable of course.

But what can you donate seven months later?

Can you donate my friend back her job? She lost it because the company she works for was downsizing due to storm damage.

Can you donate a conscience to this other company who fired my other friend because they wanted to hire someone for less to cut costs?

Can you donate understanding and compassion to business owners who don't live here and think their employees should be operating at full mental capacity by now?

Can you donate vacations to everyone so they can see trees again?

Can you donate a soul to those charging three times the normal amount for rent?

Can you donate a house to my neighbor next door? It's completely gone, like completely and totally gone.

Can you donate a fence to my neighbor down the road? The insurance company wouldn't give them enough for a new fence. Their two dogs keep getting loose and they chase me while I'm walking to pick up my kids from school. We're on a first name basis now.

Can you donate some sand to fill our shorelines at the bay? I can't let my kids play down there because the metal storm wall is poking through.

Can you donate the light back into my peoples' eyes?

Can you donate some shade? It's heating up faster here thanks to the lack of trees.

Can you donate enough childcare slots? Most people are still on a waiting list as many places have not reopened.

Can you donate more property adjusters and contractors? Everyone is backed up.

Can you pay off everyone's loans they took out to get work done on their homes because the insurance companies wouldn't pay up?

Can you donate a stay on hurricane season? We only have one shelter right now for a city of 100,000.

Can you donate a heart to the people in Washington who hold our lives in their hands?

Can you donate a hope for the future?

Can you donate perseverance and strength?

Can you donate a roof for my neighbors?

Can you donate walls to my friends?

What can you donate?

I wish I knew.

Can you donate the pieces my town needs to be whole?

Can you donate the years of memories that were taken away in one day?

Can you donate peace of mind?

I wish you could.

I wish what we needed could be donated.

We appreciate the thoughts and the love, even if it can't rebuild our town.

Each of us as human beings has a responsibility to reach out to help our brothers and sisters affected by disasters. One day it may be us or our loved ones needing someone to reach out to help.

— *MICHAEL W. HAWKINS*

IN A MOMENT

In a moment, things can change.

Calm seas turn angry.

Once gentle breezes howl in blinding gusts.

Rolling clouds extinguish the light of day.

In a moment, we can change.

Battered and bruised, we survive.

Shocked and shaken, we emerge.

In that moment, everything changed.

And we knew.

Deep inside, we knew.

We'd never be the same.

—Jennifer N. Fenwick, June 27, 2019

Photo by Terry Kelly/Shutterstock

MERCY CHEFS: THE MISSION OF CHEF GARY AND ANN LEBLANC

by Linda Artman

The name suggests that food is involved in a place or time where it is sorely needed. You would be correct in assuming that as truth. As you read this, you will find out that the continuing—and growing—story of Mercy Chefs is so much more. And this story cannot help but touch your heart. It is also a very important part of Panama City's story of the aftermath of Hurricane Michael.

Mercy Chefs had its beginning in the aftermath of a different hurricane—Hurricane Katrina, which devasted Louisiana in 2005.

Gary LeBlanc saw his home broken and bleeding because of Katrina and the massive flooding the storm incited. As an established chef with a satisfying career, he decided to offer help in feeding the hungry folks who desperately needed food for their survival. He saw that food was being distributed, but it wasn't being done with passion for the people or the food, concern for safety, or planning for efficiency and presentation. Gary felt led to lend his expertise and experience to help the effort.

He was so completely dedicated to this cause, that he spent many sleepless nights filling notebook after notebook with ideas and ways to implement them. When he presented what he had developed to the people in charge of the operation, he was told that it wouldn't work because it was just too difficult and too expensive to be possible.

Mercy Chefs founders, Chef Gary and Ann Leblanc. Photo by Linda Artman

Gary and his wife Ann continued to think about the issues involved and devised plans to make it possible and practical to give hungry people needed sustenance following natural disasters in their communities. Whenever or wherever it was so bad that local organizations and volunteers could not manage what was needed, they formulated a way to provide life-saving food in caring, creative and loving ways.

Just two weeks before Gary's 50th birthday, they began to execute the plan that completely changed the path of their life together. They have also forever changed the people around them who feel the impact of their loving purpose. These humble beginnings and this basic premise became the foundation for Mercy Chef's and their t motto: FEEDING BODY AND SOUL.

The first time their plans were put to the test was during deployment to Conklin, NY, following a flood. It was a family affair. The LeBlanc children, aged 6 and 9 at that time, were an integral part of their outreach team. Both the kids, who are young adults now and very involved in the Mercy Chefs organization, remember that they shucked pallet after pallet of sweet corn in a seemingly endless contribution to the effort! Lessons learned by each member of the family helped them refine their plan and strengthen their resolve to continue in the direction God was leading them

Mercy Chefs grew very slowly at first—and that was a good thing. Neither Gary nor Ann had experience in fundraising, so they simply charged all of the expenses on their personal credit cards. When they got back from a deployment, Gary wrote letters to everyone he knew and everyone he could think of that might help with the project. When it got bigger and more difficult to get money from friends and family, they realized that they needed help and a better plan.

The changes growth has been astounding. Just three-and-a-half years ago Chef Gary LeBlanc was the head of the organization with the help of a part-time assistant. Today there are sixteen permanent staff, including three staff chefs and twelve to eighteen volunteer chefs who work intermittently as needed. The paid staff are joined at each deployment or permanent site by a veritable army of volunteers. Mercy Chefs considers their volunteers the lifeblood of the operation. Staffing the facilitates and the prep and serving the meals are done by the many volunteers who are always ready to help.

Mercy Chefs has deployed to more than seven foreign countries (including Haiti, Nepal, Zimbabwe, Guatemala, and the Philippines), twenty-four sates, and Puerto Rico. There are permanent Mercy Chefs kitchens established in Haiti and Puerto Rico. Locals have been trained and are able to continue the outreach largely on their own.

There is also a community kitchen in Virginia, established by Mercy Chefs. Children from low income families who are "food insecure" eat meals there. They and their families are part of an extended education program intended to show them how to eat healthily at very low cost. The Lonesome Dove Ranch in Texas is a summer outreach camp established and run by Mercy Chefs for kids in the foster care system. With the "teach a man to fish" principle at work—many people benefit countless ways.

When asked about where things are going in 5-10 years, Chef Gary laughed his wonderfully deep, contagious laugh and said, "I'm afraid to put things like that in words or on paper because things are happening so fast, I'm afraid it'll happen tomorrow! It's like riding a wild pony. You just hold on and see where you go!" Several things that he's seen as future goals have already come to fruition due to needs recognized—and Mercy Chefs' ability and availability to work things out.

Funding is still a big part of the story. About 93% of expenses are met through private donations. As the reputation of the organization grows and the original mission is expanded in such positive ways, Mercy Chefs has garnered some corporate sponsorships. Increased donations in both areas would help as funding is the only real obstacle they face, according to Chef Gary. The importance of being good stewards of monies donated is at the forefront of decision-making. For the ability to feed bodies and souls and to continue to honor the hearts of donors, the funding must be used wisely.

Now that you have an idea what Mercy Chefs is about, it is important to understand what all that means to Bay County.

Hurricane Michael was big and bad. He left behind a trail of devastation as he raged through the Florida Panhandle and on into Georgia. The damage was so complete that there was no way for local organizations to meet the needs of the people left in the rubble. It was just the situation that speaks to the heart of Mercy Chefs—and they have answered that call in big ways.

Only a few short days after the storm, the caravan of trucks and the big white trailer full of ovens and equipment struggled through blocked roads, tried out a temporary site and finally found its "home away from home" in the parking lot of Emerald Coast Fellowship in Lynn Haven.

A few days after Michael, Mercy Chef's arrived in Panama City. They've returned many times since to provide meals and to spread hope. Photo by Linda Artman

Many of the staff had not been home for two months because of hurricanes in the Carolinas and Texas. Their deployments followed closely one after the other. Despite missing homes and families, these tired but dedicated workers provided food to more than 2,000 people each day.

The people came, telling their frightening stories of living through Michael, and they left with amazing food, plus the knowledge that people cared and had shared their love and hope for a better future. ALL of that was needed more than ever before.

Normally, Mercy Chefs provides food for the immediate needs of the people and leaves after three or four days, or as soon as local people and programs can take over. They stayed at the Lynn Haven site for three weeks, knowing that the infrastructure of the area could not provide what their organization was giving. The void left by Mercy Chefs' departure after only three days would have been impossibly large. They felt they just had to stay.

Another factor played a big part in the decision to remain. The staff and traveling volunteers who came with them found the people of Bay County to be incredibly resilient, hardworking, and generous beyond belief. Many who worked for hours in the heat to help feed those arriving alone or in groups had lost much—or everything—themselves. They were reaching out to others even in the midst of their own incredible need.

Neighbors were helping neighbors everywhere. People came to get meals for friends, family, and strangers who didn't have means to come themselves. They told of areas still blocked by fallen trees and downed wires and asked if they could help by getting food to those folks. And they came back day after day, meal after meal, to do what they could to help. They helped Mercy Chefs' staff to identify areas that needed delivered meals and the caravan of Mercy Chefs vehicles set out to feed even more bodies and souls.

It is difficult to articulate the feelings—which quickly became heartfelt connections—on both sides. Those serving and those receiving each felt deeply the impact of the daily interactions. Obviously, the very mission of Mercy Chefs was being accomplished on the food side of the line. The spoken appreciation for the quality of the food—many times in great surprise—and the immense gratitude for having both physical and emotional needs met was incredibly sincere and noticeably heartfelt from the receiving side. Nowhere before had feelings run so deep. Nowhere before had the devastation been so complete. The effects of the storm and the grateful, generous people on both sides of the human equation solidified a lifetime relationship and furnished countless memories.

In response to comments of how good the food looked and tasted, Chef Gary said, "We don't do chainsaws and debris removal, so the food just HAS to be amazing!" That explains a great deal about his unwavering commitment to quality and love. Seeing Panama City folks helping each other in so many ways made the LeBlanc's and their team feel that they just HAD to work alongside them.

Thus began a continuing resolve by Mercy Chefs and the local volunteers who supported them to extend a helping hand over a longer period of time, and in doing so, to become an important part of Panama City's recovery efforts.

They returned at Thanksgiving with traditional turkey and dressing meals to bring just a tiny bit of normalcy to the hurting population. They came again for all of March to feed the students who wouldn't have lunches at school during spring break and the college students who used their spring break time to help with recovery. When they came in March, they rolled into town and set up that big kitchen-on-wheels in a different church parking lot. This time it was St Andrews Baptist, but many of the faces were the same—both staff and volunteers. The need TO help was nearly as great as the need FOR help.

The latest Mercy Chefs effort in Panama City is the longest and biggest. Because there are approximately 5,000 students who are classified as homeless in Bay County School District, and because many are part of financially struggling families due to damages caused by Hurricane Michael, Mercy Chefs came back again—with plans to stay all summer long. The mission this time—to serve all the students of Bay County and their families so that kids missing school lunches while school isn't in session don't go to bed hungry.

During each of their visits, Mercy Chefs has prepared and served over 2,000 meals daily.
Photo by Linda Artman

Families were lovingly registered and then cared for and served six dinners/week from the end of school in the beginning of June through the start of school in August. Bay County Schools agreed to let Mercy Chefs use the mothballed Oscar Patterson School. There is a full kitchen in which to create the dinners, a steam table from which to serve, and real plates to put on tables that are complete with centerpieces! The idea is that the families can come to enjoy a meal and each other's company in a place removed from the distractions of leaky roofs, bare studs with no drywall, and fights with insurance companies. They aren't all crammed together in a tent or a small trailer. As families came to dine each evening they saw other families and begin to recognize them as the days and weeks passed—thus meeting a secondary goal—to build a sense of community in a natural, comfortable way.

The outreach doesn't stop there. At their own expense, Mercy Chefs began to repurpose classrooms. The first rooms were outfitted to house the staff that would be there the whole summer as well as those who would rotate in and out of the facility. And STILL they kept going—until they had bunk rooms enough to accommodate up to 100 volunteers. There are church and youth groups and other organizations who came to help in Panama City, could not find affordable places to stay. Mercy Chefs provides a place with their bunk rooms and fed the volunteers, too!

As a volunteer myself, I can tell you that these goals were already being met by the end of the first week. In the beginning families came in, sat at tables away from others, finished quickly and left. By the end of that week, many were lingering over their meals, kids were creating together on the long table in the cafeteria covered with art supplies, and everywhere you looked there were visible signs of contentment. Families were seeing familiar faces, saying hello, and joining each other at tables to eat together. It was wonderful to be a part of that community. It was wonderful to see the hard work of so many bringing about the intended results.

The effort in Panama City isn't Mercy Chefs "first rodeo." They have accomplished many things around the world and have refined and expanded their model. The people of Panama City have been the fortunate recipients of the incredible commitment to quality and love that is the cornerstone of the organization and the outreach it provides.

Mercy Chefs has made a very positive impact on the grateful people they've lovingly served in Bay County. When they leave, they will take with them lasting memories, and those of us who shared a time and place with the good people of Mercy Chefs in whatever way we participated, will forever bask in the glow of the experience.

◆ ◆ ◆

NOTHING OF STRENGTH

The evening after,

the sun set

with a resounding orange,

that set fire to what remained.

Broken trees. Barren roads.

The shattering complete.

I thought I was strong.

Until I saw the young boy,

standing before what used to be

his home. "It's all gone, he said

with trembling voice.

"But, I'm still here."

That's when I knew.

I knew nothing of strength at all.

— Jennifer N. Fenwick, April 15, 2019

Sights like this one are still visible throughout the region, even a year after Michael. Navigating the insurance and government bureaucracies has become a different kind of storm for many. Image by Terry Kelley/Shutterstock

BROKEN AND GROWING

The death toll was low
Unless we consider your kinfolk
Too many to count
Takes our breath away
You barely survived
Wind whipped
Your arms torn away
Torso cracked
Heart broken
Not a willow yet we see your sticky tears
All that remains is a sickening stump
jagged and jarring
We should put you out of your misery
Call Bob
That cat can do the job
Wait
What's this?
A tiny bud
It's not spring
You're confused
Or in shock
Maybe both
We thought we'd lost you
But
You're blooming out of season
You're putting all your energy into
the promise of tomorrow
Is this a last hoorah or a full recovery?
Hard to know
Either way
It's beautiful and bold
Broken and growing
That's what you are
You're not alone
Show us the way

— *Jason Hedden, March 5, 2019*

Jennifer N. Fenwick

Photo by Jason Hedden

FOREVER CHANGED CONTINUES

by Jane Smith

Here we are almost a year after the onslaught and destruction of Hurricane Michael. The chapter I wrote in *In the eye of the Storm*, was entitled "Forever Changed," and unfortunately that still holds true today.

Our home and belongings were destroyed, and we literally had to rebuild from the ground up. I am hoping and praying our new house will be completed within the next month or so. What would normally have taken 6 months to build has stretched into possibly a year or more due to an extremely limited work force.

We were fortunate to receive a FEMA camper, but that in no way compares to a real home. One doesn't fully appreciate the conveniences of an actual home until they don't have one. The electric bill is outrageous because the AC doesn't stop, and every little thing—like the microwave and blow dryer—causes the breaker to trip and requires a trip out to the power pole.

Cooking is basically nonexistent because of the heat, so most meals consist of take out. My dear husband makes a weekly trip to the laundromat. Not only have we suffered, but so many pets were affected as well. Originally our yard was fenced in, and our 5 fur babies could come and go as they pleased.

In and out the doggie door. They made the transition to a small pen in the yard. Unfortunately due to the high temps we had this summer, we did lose one of our precious dogs to heat stroke. It's so

Charles and Jane Smith stand on the porch of their new home, still under construction almost a year after Hurricane Michael destroyed their house. Little things like the day the drywall went up and the day their new front door was mounted bring joy. Photo by Jane Smith

very sad, that we are almost at the one year anniversary, and yet there is still so much to be done. There are homes still in rubble, numerous homes that have been demolished, and the ever present blue tarps.

The stress from the past year has been hard on everyone, but especially me. Besides losing our home, our precious dog, and our almost losing our son from a dangerous bacteria, it was discovered recently that after being in remission from breast cancer for 8 years, the beast has returned, this time in my bone and colon.

I began treatment for the bone cancer several weeks ago, and will undergo surgery in a couple weeks to hopefully remove the cancer in my colon. Stress is a huge factor as far as cancer is concerned and I was so physically and emotionally exhausted from all the hits in the past year, my body just couldn't fight it any longer.

When I titled the chapter in our first book, "Forever Changed" little did I know that this would truly mean forever. It is my hope and prayer, that I am successful beating this beast, and that I will be around for many more years—to continue to add chapters.

FAREWELL, MICHAEL

Michael,
I refuse to let you occupy so many of my thoughts any longer.
You took from me memories,
belongings, and precious keepsakes,
some that belonged to my grandmother.
When we have storms now,
we are immediately taken back
to that horrible day so many of us
didn't think we would make it through.
I have sat and dreamt for almost a year now,
about being back in a real house,
sitting on a real couch,
sleeping in a real bed,
and cooking a real meal.
It actually looks like that will soon become a reality.
You were not particular on who chose to ravish.
We adults coped somewhat better,
but our poor children that went through this will remain fragile.
I have allowed you in a way,
to occupy my thoughts for way to long now.
As my new house nears completion,
I choose to bid you a farewell,
and begin a new chapter without you— hopefully a distant memory.

— Jane Smith, August 29, 2019

RECOVERY

by Thomas H. Cook

September 4, 2019—It was 320 days ago when all of our lives were forever changed here in the Greater Panama City area. Still today, you can ride up and down many streets and see homes and businesses that still look like they did on the evening of October 10, 2018.

Devastation is still all around. Big trucks are still hauling debris to large processing areas to be ground down into smaller chips in order to be hauled to the local landfills. Local governments have had to keep pushing out debris pick up deadlines because of the sheer volume that still remains to be cleaned up and removed.

Neighborhoods that were once were filled with large lush beautiful oak trees, magnolias, and pines now look like a scene from a 1950's nuclear testing site. Gone are century old oaks that were plentiful before the storm

Shredded blue tarps flap in the breeze as they have deteriorated from covering hundreds of roofs over the past 10 months that are still waiting repair or demolition.

Most locals now flinch whenever an afternoon thunderstorm rolls though, and the wind blows hard. The sound of the rain and wind causes distress to many for various reasons. For some, it's because their home is still leaking and in disrepair, for others, it's a reminder of the hours they spent in a closet or other small space with a mattress on top of them while listening to the howling wind and the deafening sound of their home disintegrating around them all while praying that they would live to see another day.

Untold numbers of people are still fighting with insurance and casualty companies on a daily basis to be made whole from a policy they have paid premiums on for years on end only to be treated less than human when filing a claim.

Many people have had to just walk away from their homes and jobs and leave the area in order to find affordable housing. For what little apartments and homes that are now available for rent, the prices are way above the average family's income, placing a huge financial burden on those people seeking affordable housing

Employers all across town are having trouble filling open positions because so many people have had to leave the area in order to find affordable homes along with new jobs.

We still have one of the largest hospitals in our area operating at just one tenth of their overall operating capacity because the storm caused an estimated 40 million dollars in damage to the facility. Since the storm, they had to lay off over 800 employees.

Our school system has also suffered tremendously. There is well over 300 million dollars' worth of damage to facilities all around the county. Many schools were so badly damaged that they have been closed indefinitely. Recently, it was reported that nearly every school in Bay County will require a new roof due to the damage caused by Michael. It is estimated that it will take 10 years or more before our school system will be back to a pre-Hurricane status.

The people of the Florida Panhandle are hardworking and caring folks and we will rebuild and recover. On October 10th, 2018, all of our lives were forever changed. That day, we became category 5 survivors.

◆ ◆ ◆

SO MANY STORIES

by Jennifer N. Fenwick

"Nearly five months after Hurricane Michael ravaged the Florida Panhandle, economic setbacks and delays have made recovery increasingly difficult for Florida Panhandle residents trying to rebuild their homes, and their lives." — Allie Raffa, Fox News, 28 FEB 2019

March 1, 2019—When I set out to capture the stories of Hurricane Michael across the Panhandle, I never anticipated the impact, *In the Eye of the Storm*, would have on the region devastated by the October 10, 2018 monster storm. It started out as a way for survivors to share their stories, their grief, and heartbreak, and their hopes for the future.

In the weeks since *In the Eye of the Storm: Stories of Survival and Hope from the Florida Panhandle* was published; the outpouring of support and engagement has been humbling.

"We need more people like you," said Tina Rudisill in a message she sent me via social media after purchasing two copies of the book, one for her and one for a friend. "You can show the world our journey."

Rudisill and her husband, both disabled, rode out the Category 5 storm in their home in Panama City. "We lost everything but our lives," she explained. "We had just bought our home two years ago and it is devasting seeing everything destroyed."

Rudisill is not alone in her grief. There are so many stories like hers across the region. So many I wish I could have included in the book. So many that deserve to be shared. As I continue to meet people, to listen to their voices, to provide comfort where I can, I'm inspired to continue this journey.

"Perhaps a follow-up book will come out of this," I told Rudisill in my reply to her message, "An anniversary edition marking one-year following the storm. Stories of progress and hope in the aftermath."

"Oh my goodness," she immediately responded, "What an awesome idea. A follow-up of healing and starting over is so needed for the communities impacted."

"It pulls at the heart strings to hear from other people that survived the storm and to hear their stories of strength and moving forward after such major devastation to this area. Anyone that doesn't know or isn't struggling to come back from this storm really needs to read this," wrote an Amazon reviewer on 24 FEB 2019.

Readers have embraced our stories. Their kind words and heartfelt reviews have comforted us as we move forward on this unexpected journey.

Our book is not the only one telling the stories of the heartbreak of the people living in the aftermath of this historic storm. *Survivors: Work Created in the Wake of Hurricane Michael,* released on November 20, 2018, is a collection of poems, essays, short stories, artwork, and images compiled by Tony Simmons of the Panama City News Herald and local artist, Jayson Kretzmer.

Mike Caz Cazalas, also from the News Herald, produced a beautiful book of compelling photographs and newspaper front page stories documenting Michael's impact across the Panhandle. *Michael* is a collector's item that will forever commemorate October 10th and the immediate weeks following the storm. A portion of the proceeds from both of these publications are being donated to the Hurricane Michael Relief Fund to assist with rebuilding across the region.

Memoirs of Michael—The Hurricane is a Facebook page dedicated to sharing survivor stories. The page, created by Ashley Conner and Photographer, Cierra Camper, tells the stories of the men and women who survived Michael and are committed to rebuilding their communities.

October 10, 2018 is a day the Florida Panhandle will never forget. The day, our lives and our cities were dramatically altered, irrevocably and forever. Compiling the stories, poetry, and images submitted for this project was raw and real.

I realized going in, what a huge undertaking and responsibility this task was. I also realized that we could not tell every story; and there were thousands and thousands. What we hoped instead, was that the stories we were able to tell would resonate, and that in doing so, *In the Eye of the Storm*, would become a voice for the region.

The latest statistics on Hurricane Michael place property damage throughout the Panhandle at $5 billion with a $1.5 billion loss in crops, and $1.3 billion in timber. "This is going to be a long, long recovery," Senator Bill Montford told the Tallahassee Democrat a few days following the storm. Photo by Shutterstock

SMALL SIGNS

Small signs of hope,

renewal, and faith.

In the aftermath of the storm,

this is all we have.

In the midst of the chaos,

this is what we cling to.

In the face of an uncertain future,

this is what sustains us.

— Jennifer N. Fenwick, April 4, 2019

Signs of Hope. Photo by Tony Miller

BEHIND THE SCENES OF MERCY CHEFS: BEACON OF HOPE

by Linda Artman

As Mercy Chefs has grown, so has the number of people who have become dedicated to feeding the bodies and souls that are left in areas following natural disasters. Founders, Gary LeBlanc and his wife Ann, were the actual genesis of Mercy Chefs and are still at the core of the organization. They are the kind of people who simply radiate love and concern for others. It is deeply felt by anyone they come in contact with, and it draws like-minded folks to become part of what they do. There is a feeling of willing servitude in everyone who becomes a part of the operation. Staff and volunteers alike. It's just there. Everyday. It shines through heat, cold, exhaustion, irritation, or anxiety. It is what gets everyone through rough, long days. Loving, willing servitude IS Mercy Chefs.

Ray LeBlanc was the six-year-old corn shucker of the very first deployment. That was when the entire young LeBlanc family went to help after storm waters flooded the town of Conklin, NY. It was the first step of Ray's participation in a way of life that has come to help define who he is as a young adult.

Nearly every holiday break from school was spent on the road with the family and the growing mission of Mercy Chefs. Thanksgivings and Christmases meant helping prepare and serve literally thousands of turkeys, plus all the trimmings—since disaster areas were frequently revisited during the holidays as a morale booster.

Ray LeBlanc, son of Mercy Chef's founders, Gary and Ann LeBlanc. Photo by Linda Artman

Megan LeBlanc, Ray's older sister, was the nine-year-old corn shucker in Conklin, NY. They frequently participated in the mission by having one or both of their parents absent due to deployments. In a very real way they contributed even when they didn't actually go on a deployment. Ray understood the reason behind the absences, and because of that, he accepted the situation as a necessary function of his father's job. As he got older and became very involved in baseball, basketball and football, the family did everything possible to make it work for him to participate. That's when big sister Megan really stepped up. She was often the one who packed his lunches and helped with homework. Ray remembers that it was all done with much love. "I'd be a very different person today if not for Megan." It is evident that she holds a very special and important place in his heart. Today, Megan is director of social media for Mercy Chefs.

When asked what he sees when he looks at his parents and realizes what they have done with and through Mercy Chefs, Ray was obviously proud. He recognized their efforts to balance family with the growing responsibilities they dealt with due to the ever-greater outreach. He is impressed with what his dad has built from such humble beginnings. This summer, with the extended time in Panama City, Ray has a more professional, administrative role through which he works closely with his parents.

"Being able to pick their brains and learn every day from their experience and expertise is wonderful. I'm thankful every day!" This has given him a different perspective and deeper understanding of what his parents have accomplished. He sees a different side of them, and that has made him even prouder.

Hannah Saylor got involved with Mercy Chefs through family, too. Her mom began working as a chef for the organization after tornadoes struck Moore, OK, and soon Hannah found herself part of the mission, by volunteering in the mobile kitchen. She often worked when her mom was in areas close to home, but disasters come where they come, and her mom had to go to them. In fact, Mom, Chef Lisa, was in Panama City after Hurricane Michael for Hannah's 21st Birthday. A large group of staff and volunteers took a break on the serving line to sing happy birthday on a FaceTime call. It helped ease the sadness of the separation for both of them on such a big day— And it strengthened the feeling of family to all who participated.

This summer Hannah has a larger responsibility as a staff member for the Panama City operation. She is the On-site Project Manager.

As a nursing student, she has a serving heart, but this year she has taken a big step and committed her entire summer break to working with Mercy Chefs. She left her friends and all of their plans because she felt led to do this job. She appreciates the fact that people saw in her the ability and capability to meet the challenges. She understands at a much deeper level what Mercy Chefs is all about. Seeing a bigger picture has made it clear how and why decisions are made to further the mission of the organization. She admits that it has become dearer to her heart as time passes.

"Your heart can't stay out of it when it's 24/7 for nine whole weeks!"

Mercy Chefs volunteers turned staff, Emily Enyeart and Hannah Saylor. Photo by Linda Artman

Hannah is invested more than ever. The day she began working at the school building in Panama City housing Beacon of Hope, she met many of the people she would be working with for the very first time. Not only that, but they would also be living together in the classrooms they were turning into bunk rooms. It really is 24/7. Their shared commitment to the mission has brought them close together in friendship as well. Hannah says that having everyone around means she's never lonely, and there is always someone to do things with on the one day off they have each week. Alone time can also be carved out in the mornings or when going to the gym after the dinner service. There is community and courtesy among the now close friends.

The responsibilities of being project manager are many and varied. Among many other things, she helped organize and build the bunk rooms, established activities and an art table for the kids coming to dinner, and worked at the registration table making certain that a Bay County student was among the groups arriving. The latter sometimes exposed Hannah to people who were upset with the new "rules" governing participation in this particular outreach. Always before, Mercy Chefs gave everyone who came a meal—and sent as many home as they said they needed. This time having a student in a Bay County school was required. That led to some big frustrations, especially during the beginning week. Most of the time Hannah was able to kindly smile it away using her natural Southern Charm. As people began to better understand the program, that part of the job got easier.

As things settled in and routines developed, Hannah has come to realize how grateful she is for having the opportunity to serve here with both the people she works with and the folks she helps serve through her role with Mercy Chefs.

"The very heart of Mercy Chefs is the way it continues to call out the best in people—regardless of their circumstances or place in life."

Mercy Chef staff member, Stephen Bradshaw. Photo by Linda Artman

Stephen Bradshaw has been a part of disaster relief for sixteen years. His first experience with rescue work was as a first responder. His call to Panama City after Hurricane Michael was for security in areas where law enforcement needed some auxiliary help. As he provided that at Mercy Chefs sites during all the deployments made to Panama City, the leaders of the organization and Stephen realized that he should be a permanent, full-time staffer. Now he deploys to each site Mercy Chefs serves and helps establish the effort. The security job has turned Stephen into a jack-of-all-trades—and has even had him at the stove more than once! His quiet, kind way of dealing with contentious situations has defused many interactions that could easily have escalated into bigger problems. He sometimes looks serious and stern, but those who know him recognize in his big heart the same willing servitude found in others who give themselves to this mission.

Stephen remarked that the destruction caused by Michael is the worst he has seen in all his years of being called to disaster areas. The area affected is so big and the damage so widespread that it is hard to fathom. As they sit in the courtyard outside their bunk room, the evening breezes often still carry the sounds of gas generators. People are still living in tents and trailers—still trying to recover. Stephen says that the difficulties and frustrations in all of that have intensified drug problems in the area. Some who were on the edge were pushed over it. His security position has made him feel very profoundly the responsibility for the safety of all who are staying in the bunk rooms. Mercy Chefs was able to hire off-duty police officers to help with that over weekends, but Stephen patrols the area the rest of the week just to make sure no unauthorized people come onto the property during the night.

"I'm used to deploying to natural disasters, so there's really been no change in that since I began with Mercy Chefs, but sometimes I miss the rescue end of it." Mercy Chefs rescues thousands in more indirect ways, and Stephen is a big part of that.

Emily Enyeart grew up pretty sheltered in a very small town in Virginia. After graduating from the Culinary Institute of Virginia, two major opportunities demanded a choice be made. Should she accept employment at Walt Disney World? Or should she become a chef with

Mercy Chefs? Working at Mercy Chefs would allow her much more control and input, but working at Disney—!

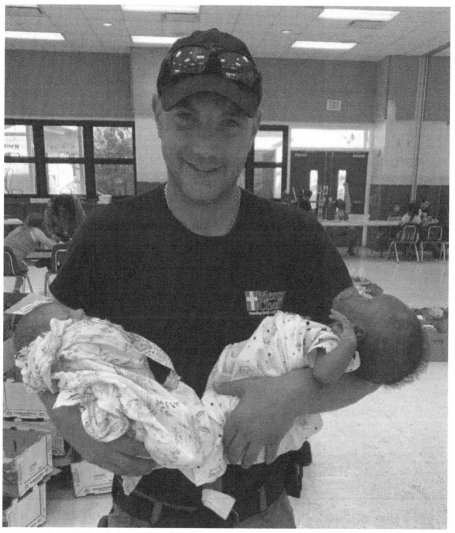

Stephen Bradshaw is Mercy Chef's Jack-of-all-trades, which includes nursery provider when needed. Photo by Linda Artman

One of Emily's instructors—and a great mentor—had recently begun work with Mercy Chefs, and that helped make the decision easier. Soon Chef Emily found herself working in the community kitchen helping families with food insecurities find healthy ways to stretch their meager food budgets. Thus began her journey discovering the joys of cooking with a purpose.

She has now been part of Mercy Chefs' deployments in addition to her responsibilities with the community kitchen and has been the managing chef, gaining valuable experience. She has not regretted her choice to walk away from the Disney opportunity. This is real and fulfilling. There is such variety and opportunity for growth that she can see a long-term relationship developing.

As an intermittent part of the summer-long program in Panama City, Chef Emily has seen firsthand the combination of community outreach and disaster relief that is Beacon of Hope. She has lived 24/7 with her coworkers while staying at the school. She says that it has been easy to make things work in this situation because all of their hearts and minds are on the big picture, seeing what the project means to the people they serve every day. Each brings something unique that makes it work.

At the center of Emily's determination is her passion for food and bringing education to food service. This is her first real experience with the "God part" according to her account. Every day brings new ways to learn. She is seeing clearly how that part fits into Mercy Chefs' mission. She sees staff caring about each other as they care for the victims of Michael and his awful aftermath. She has evidenced the sadness and loss the people have faced through their stories. She has also witnessed the fact that there can be moments of joy and happiness over meals together.

"We all have food in common, and we all share things over and through food. I learned to cook in culinary school, but with Mercy Chefs I have learned what it feels like to cook with purpose and love."

Lisa Saylor, "Mom" to Program Director, Hannah, is a giant part of the HEART of Mercy Chefs. She is so full of love that it positively overflows through her warm smile and the bright pink streak in her hair. Lisa is the first to admit that she doesn't travel light to any deployment! She shows up in her converted blood mobile bus complete with her dog and enough décor to make any site "homey!" Her claim is to "self-monitored high maintenance." Her food is amazing, her desserts, legendary. Everyone who has ever shared work with her has gone away richer from the experience.

Chef Lisa of Mercy Chefs. Photo by Linda Artman

Chef Lisa began as a volunteer with Mercy Chefs in Oklahoma. She went to help a church that was hosting a post-disaster food site.

After getting information about Mercy Chefs, she went home, got clothes, and stayed. She was mesmerized by the idea that such a great meal could come in a foam box. She was already a chef and had her own catering company, but this was different.

"From a culinary standpoint, this was IT! I was so excited to be able to use my culinary gifts to be a part of Mercy Chefs. Having deep human compassion in these situations has lead me to feel ownership of others' pain and suffering and because of that, I am drawn to help."

And help she has. Among the long list of accomplishments since her start, Chef Lisa has deployed more than 50 times, has fed other disaster aid groups countless numbers of times, been part of Summer of Hope in Baltimore 6-8 times, and run the Lonesome Dove Ranch in Texas for kids in the foster care system. (She says she will be part of that summer program until they don't let her anymore!)

This is Lisa's fourth time to deploy to Panama City. She feels such a pull to work with and for these people. In all the places she's gone to help, Panama City has the strongest pull on her heart. She's seen folks volunteering despite having lost everything themselves. She's seen a depth of gratitude that touches her heart. She's seen a devastating destruction that is unmatched in any other area. And, yet, the people of Panama City are resilient and positive. They just keep working HARD toward the new version of themselves and the town they lovingly call home.

Panama City has been deeply blessed by the presence of each of these incredibly talented and loving individuals and by the amazing Mercy Chefs organization as a whole. There are many personal stories not told here. There are many more staff and volunteers who are an integral part of the operation who are not mentioned. The reader should understand that there are MANY behind the scenes that make Mercy Chefs the exemplary, global outreach organization that touches hearts through the food it provides in times and places of great need. **WE IN BAY COUNTY ARE ETERNALLY GRATEFUL**.

THE WEDDING DRESS

by Dr. Amy Boe

July 29, 2019—We went back to Panama City this weekend so Daniel could spend his 14th birthday with friends. Since October we have tried our best to ensure the kids are able to still enjoy mission trips, youth camps, birthdays, D-NOW, prom, and graduations—all the things that were so dramatically taken away from them by Hurricane Michael.

It's been hard traveling that much, but I am happy we were able to do that for them. It has been worth it. After all the trips, camps, and parties, it is hard for them to leave their friends. We understand that. We try to make it as positive as possible and it is getting easier for them. Bethany even commented yesterday that it was the first time she actually felt like she was going "home" when we left for Birmingham. That gave me so much relief. As a parent, the last thing you want is for your child to be in pain.

Yesterday before we left Panama City, we went by the house to gather some more belongings. I always try to avoid 390 until I absolutely have to go to our house. I just do not want to see it, but this was our last day so—it was time.

I don't know why but as it is finally getting easier and easier for the kids to visit and leave again, it is getting harder and harder for me. I suppose in a lot of ways I was initially in shock—as everyone was. I honestly had no 'feeling' for the first several months after the storm. I could not cry, I did not feel sad, just kind of numb.

Now, almost ten months later, I can't help but feel sad constantly and cry uncontrollably, especially as I look at it, in person. It's all part of the grieving process, I guess. So many memories as I drove into the driveway yesterday, yet, not at all what I want to see—grass hip high, porch dilapidated, holes in walls, unpleasant smells—no life—to what once was a very happy place. I want to only remember the good things—of the kids running down the stairs at Christmas, Bethany going on her first date, the look in Daniel's eyes when I walked in the living room as he had managed to empty an entire (Sam's size) jar of peanut butter on his face, ladies Bible studies, youth swim parties, India planning meetings—the love and laughter, I remember so well. It makes me smile through the tears.

I spotted the box that contained my wedding dress back in November. It was trapped under the stairs with big brown water spots all over it. Even though the closet is in the center of the house, it managed to get drenched with rain. I told myself the dress was ruined, and I could not bring myself to open it and look at it. I just didn't know if I could stand to see it. Every time we went home to salvage what we could, I would see it—and look away. So crazy that out of all the things we lost in the storm that one thing would make such a difference.

Steve went ahead of the kids and me to begin loading the trailer. When I walked in—there was "the" box. The one I had been ignoring and too afraid to open. This time it wasn't in the closet, but right in the middle of the living room floor. Steve was emptying out the closet and pulled it out. I guess this was going to be the day I would muster up the emotional energy to face the dress. So, I did.

I think I must have held my breath as I opened it slowly. Part of me wanted to take it back to the closet and abandon it altogether. Just forget about it forever—yeah, I could do that. But, no. I didn't. I followed through and to my amazement there was not one, single, tiny watermark on it!! It was perfect!! I couldn't believe what my eyes were telling me! Of course, I cried—I think mostly out of all the adrenaline that immediately left my body, but still—WOW!

As I looked it over, careful not to let it touch the filthy floor, I couldn't help but think of the powerful picture of the Church in the world—What a breath-taking visual representation it was to me.

God reminded me yesterday that this earth is not our home. As beautiful and comfortable houses can be—they aren't forever. As there are weeds, and brokenness, shattered glass, sadness and even death, He is there, continually making His Church into the Bride she is supposed to be—"so that he might present the church to himself in splendor, without spot or wrinkle or any such thing, that she might be holy and without blemish (Eph.5.27).

When the storms come, He protects us. When the wars rage, He is there as a mighty fortress and a shield. Even when our personal boxes—that are often ignored, wear out on the outside, God is preserving for Himself a Bride! And that Bride stands in stark contrast to the world. When he sees his children compared, I can't help but believe that this picture is what he sees—a messed up, sad, world that is falling apart without him and his gorgeous Bride awaiting his return.

◆ ◆ ◆

Photo by Amy Boe

PORTABLE

Portable

How will they remove the debris they cannot see?

How would they even find it?

He'll never get it to the curb

It's far too heavy

It's hidden in his heart

and cluttering his mind

It's not a job for the grabber truck

That would surely crush him more

It may take a gentler hand

He'd ask for help but

They have enough worries of their own

and They're far too busy

Her son had his third first day of school today

He said he wasn't nervous

but he checked his bag a dozen times

Trying to control at least one thing

She dropped him off in the normal spot

but he went left not right to a collection of

temporary rooms beside the carcass of a school

She drove off then parked in a panic

She traced his path to make sure he had found his way

He was safe

She shed a tear or three

Proud that her boy had found his way

Surrounded by those that care for him like he was their own

The spray painted signs are gone

The new batch has arrived

They look like the old ones but they're just vinyl stand-ins

The illusion of wholeness

The debris is leaving but the scars remain

And those are just the ones we can see

Rain shouldn't make you cry

— Jason Hedden, January 8, 2019

Photo by Jason Hedden

I AM THANKFUL

by Thomas H. Cook

November 21, 2019—On the afternoon of October 10, 2018, Hurricane Michael came ashore along the Panhandle of Florida, with Panama City, Calloway, Lynn Haven, Parker, Tyndall AFB & Mexico Beach taking the brunt of its fury. Within a few short hours, our area was transformed from a vibrant quaint little coastal town along the Gulf Coast, to one of the top 4 worst natural disasters in the United States.

Michael has changed our community forever. Nearly every structure in town has experienced some sort of damage, from minor to catastrophic destruction. Both of our hospitals experienced catastrophic damage and the patients had to be evacuated hours after the storm and both facilities will require major renovation to bring them back to full operational capacity. Many grocery stores, gas stations and fast food places also suffered major damage, and many are still struggling to reopen, with some never to reopen again.

Many families have had to leave the area, causing a shortage of workers with many of the area's major employers across town. Many of the people left are living in homes, apartments, and other structures that are compromised, needing extensive repairs.

On the third week after the storm, I tried to put into words some of the things I was thankful for despite the situation our community is experiencing. With tomorrow being Thanksgiving, I thought I would share some of the things I am thankful for.

I am thankful that God is in control.

I am thankful that none of my family, friends, or co-workers died or suffered personal injuries. Many suffered major property damage, but material things can be replaced and rebuilt.

I am thankful for the way my community has come together to help one another in this time of need.

I am thankful that this storm hit us in late October and not the 1st of June as the heat would have been unbearable as many people were without electricity for many weeks.

I am thankful for the thousands of Electrical Linemen who left their families and worked around the clock tirelessly since the day of the storm to restore power to everyone. They accomplished an amazing feat, restoring power to most of the Panama City area within a 3-week period, after initial estimates projected restoration efforts taking several months.

I am thankful for the many Firemen, Police Officers, Sheriff Deputies, EMT's, Search and Rescue, National Guardsmen, Ambulance Drivers, First Responders, FWC Officers, and anyone else that came to our community to provide help and to provide us security—and for the ones that continue to do so.

I am thankful for our Local and State Leaders, who worked around the clock trying to restore water, sewer, trash pickup, traffic lights, and the other daily functions of local government.

I am thankful for the workers that volunteered at the shelters around town to provide for the needs of our citizens who sought shelter during and after the storm.

I am thankful that despite many of our churches being destroyed, or heavily damaged, each congregation and denomination is coming together and holding worship services in parking lots, tents, and fields. Many churches that did not sustain damage are allowing other churches to use their facilities for worship regardless of the denomination.

I am thankful for the many the people and various organizations that have been providing food, water and other necessity's around town. It's the little things that mean a lot.

I am thankful that our President and Vice President regardless of political party, have come to visit, and had the opportunity observe the damage of our community firsthand. I am thankful for their commitment to providing for the needs of our community at the federal level.

I am thankful that the federal government has committed to rebuilding Tyndall Air Force Base and is providing for the needs of our local Military families affected and displaced by the storm.

I am thankful for the many nurses and doctors and support personnel that worked around the clock at both of our hospitals to provide care to those in need; and for the many people working around the clock to restore the buildings and facilities that were so badly damaged during the storm.

I am thankful for our School Board members and Superintendent for working tirelessly to formulate a plan to return our students to school as quickly as possible. Many school facilities were heavily damaged and will require massive rebuilding.

I am thankful for the hundreds of Telecommunications workers (AT&T, Comcast, Level 3 Communications, Media Com, WOW, and Unity Fiber) that are working around the clock to restore critical communications and cell service to everyone.

I am thankful for the many local radio personalities that stayed on the air around the clock during and after the storm for days providing important information to the community concerning first aid, water, food, shelter, and providing a calming voice to those people whose only communication was a small radio for many days on end.

I am thankful that our local TV stations are back on the air and are able to provide critical information and local news again.

I am thankful for the many volunteers with chainsaws who have worked tirelessly over the past several weeks cutting and removing trees up and down nearly every street in our community.

I am thankful for the many grocery stores that are reopening and making life seem just a little bit normal again.

I could go on and on with many more things that I am thankful for, but these are some of the things that came to me as I reflected on the events that have unfolded across our community and beyond.

I am proud to be a citizen of the Panhandle and I am indeed thankful.

◆ ◆ ◆

THE PATH TO PEACE

There's a place I've been going that's just east of here
Where the beaches are white, and the water is clear.

There's just something about being in that place.
My safehouse, my refuge, my saving grace.

For moments or hours or maybe for entire days,
the destruction and blue tarps seem to all fade away.

But, as beautiful as it is and as hard as I try, I still see it.
The path.
The beginning of the eye.

I stop and pause to take a deep breath.
I remind myself of the all trees we have left.

The ones that are still alive and finally full of green.
Not the twisted and tangled ones, if you know what I mean.

If I just don't look so hard by that water tower. That's where it started.
I'm in awe of its power.

A definitive line that began the worst of its wrath
An eerily clear distinction of that dreaded path.

"How ironic?" I think as we begin to leave.
The eye of the storm is where I find the most peace.

— Teri Elizabeth Hord, August 8, 2019

Photo by Teri Elizabeth Hord

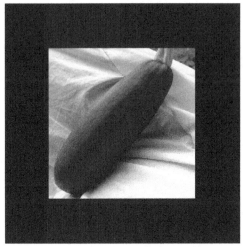

Photo by Melinda JD Hall

FIRST FRUITS

Our landscape was destroyed,

Yet death gives way to life.

First fruit from the roots of fallen,

To feed and away our strife.

— Melinda JD Hall, August 8, 2019

ALMOST

I've almost forgotten
The song of constant chainsaws
Choosing between gas or charging the phone
Seeing stars from my yard
I've almost forgotten
What used to be on that corner
Asking over and over, "Y'all okay?"
The quiver in her voice when we finally got through on broken lines
I've almost forgotten
I don't want to forget
I want to forget
I don't want to forget
I want to forget
I've almost forgotten
Almost

— *Jason Hedden, July 7, 2019*

Photo by Jason Hedden

MY SERVICE ANIMAL SAVED MY LIFE

by Elise Henkel

This is about my dog Tosha, who is a registered Service Animal who saved my life during Michael's unwelcome visit. Before I tell you how, I want to share a few things about us.

I had not taken Michael's approach seriously. My views on Michael fluctuated between a mere inconvenience to possibly an exhilarating experience. I love the water, with a lifetime of sailing, kayaking and scuba experiences. I prepared as most of us did with water, flashlights, candles, nuts, dried fruit and of course, dog food. I enjoyed a wonderful lunch the day before with a friend at a local restaurant. Four special friends called me later and offered their homes as shelter.

At the time, I thought I should stay at my condo overlooking the bay. My thoughts were nonchalant at best. Sadly in retrospect, I was also very cavalier. My flawed thinking was based on the countless blizzards, power outages, frozen pipes, hailstorms the size of golf balls, floods, avalanches, wildfires, rockslides, and winds in excess of 130 mph in Colorado that we'd endured. I thought that we could easily weather Michael. I was wrong as wrong can be. Michael changed me forever.

I first became scared when I saw 10-foot waves above the Pavilion at St. Andrews Marina where the swings are. The entire marina was flooded. I had a bird's eye view peering out from my 6th floor condo. I held Tosha in between the 'rainstorm' inside my home. I was mopping constantly using every towel I had. I did not have enough towels. My front door started to vibrate. Water was coming in there, too! I have a safety device to prop under my door handle to prevent break in's when I travel as a single woman. I propped it under the door handle. It worked. My door did not blow in it as it did for so many of my neighbors. I moved furniture, artwork, unplugged electronics, and prayed.

Elise Henkel and her best friend, Tosha, Christmas, 2018

Next, I saw the water flowing directionally from North to South with white caps of two-feet and higher. This was the first time that I witnessed an almost instantaneous, 180-degree shift of the bay water. Typically, the water flows from West to East. Now it was flowing North to South. I became terrified.

Next I saw about 20 waterspouts spiralling into the sky 50-feet and higher. Were these tornadoes or what? And then the whiteout came; all you could see was white. In Colorado, blizzards are mostly silent, with the gentle snowflakes falling like diamonds amidst glistening sunlight. However, the whiteout from Michael was not calm, peaceful or beautiful. The roar was deafening, with trees snapping like firecrackers. The boards on the dock were ripped up like toothpicks.

At this point, Tosha and I retreated to the bedroom wading through wet floors. We gazed at each other without blinking for ten minutes or more while the building began to shake and shake and shake. When would the shaking end? It seemed like an eternity. I was imaging that the two floors above us would collapse, trap, and kill us. Tosha is the love of my life, so if these were to be my last moments on earth, I was glad they'd be with this angel of God in fur.

Tosha is a Post-Traumatic Stress Disorder (PTSD) Service Animal. She kept my stress low, alerted me to dangerous increases in my blood pressure, and prevented panic attacks.

Days after the storm, I heard helicopters, the sirens of emergency vehicles, and aircraft. However, the deafening sounds of the chainsaws were the worst. Constant reminders of the devastating, catastrophic destruction. These trees were beautiful creations of God, and now they were just gone. The harmonic symphony of the birds was also gone. And then to learn about the human and pet fatalities. Could it be any worse?

I did not eat; neither did Tosha. Although neighbors gave us food, I could barely swallow. I would pet and hold Tosha for hours each day. At night, we went back to the bed and I prayed for sunlight to come soon to combat the total darkness. I felt as though I was in a daze, wondering if I was alive or in some kind of terrible nightmare. When would I wake up? Was this unreal, surreal or not real at all? When would I wake up?

I did wake up and after mandatory evacuation. Tosha and I had to go somewhere. Then the calls came in from my three sisters in Pennsylvania. They all pleaded with me to come to PA and stay with them as long as necessary. They wanted me to move there. All of them knew that I have a Service Animal. They said, no problem. I decided to take them up on the offer. It was yet another miracle. Tosha and I survived the hurricane and now my estranged sisters wanted to help me. How exhilarated I felt, after all these years my sisters do care, so I thought.

On route to Pennsylvania, I saw a caravan of specialized vehicles that were used to replace power poles piloted by linemen. I saw them even into Virginia traveling to the Panhandle. I thanked and blessed all these workers coming to help us.

I saw the train derailment on Highway 231. Banks were closed and the few that were open, had cash withdrawal limits. This reminded me of the Great Depression that my parents survived. That is how I learned to be frugal and appreciative of what I have. Again, was I dreaming?

After traveling over 1,000 miles with most of my valuables in my vehicle, in and out of hotels, terrified of driving in big cities again, I called my sister who offered to let me stay with her as long as necessary, rent free. Two hours from her house, I called so excited to be back in the picturesque rolling hills of Lancaster County. Instead of the welcome I'd expected, she said, that tonight was not a good time. I had to get a hotel, as no sister would let me stay with them. In all fairness, my sisters were dealing with significant challenges in their personal lives. Unfortunately for me, I drove with the belief that my sisters truly cared about me. After I arrived, I felt as though none of them thought it through regarding sanctuary for me and Tosha.

I talked frequently with my Florida friends on this journey. A dear friend said, 'Dorothy Come Home'. And I responded, 'Toto too'? She said, 'Tosha too'.

Another kind and generous friend and his wife offered me shelter in their beautiful retirement home in Navarre, Florida. Another miracle. I experienced many miracles during and after Michael. But the best miracle has been Tosha.

I suffered from anxiety, depression, and PTSD every moment of every hour of the day even before Michael. Unfortunately for those of us with a preexisting diagnosis of PTSD, additional catastrophic traumas compound and worsen our conditions. This illness advances exponentially with repeated trauma. In other words, my stress is 1,000 times worse. Tosha helps me 24/7. She's saved my life so many times.

I encourage those of you suffering from PTSD after the storm, to seek mental health counseling and to hold and pet an animal and kiss a plant or tree that survived. Smile at everyone you see. We are all survivors!

RISING

Yes, things have been hard.
Yes, so much has been destroyed.
So much else is just—gone.
Yes, we've been struggling.
So many pieces to pick up.
So much healing still to come.
Yes, we're still grieving.
We will continue to.
For a long time.
Because you see,
It takes more than 365 days.
More than 52 weeks,
To heal from this.
It takes a lifetime.
And even then,
long after then,
some scars will remain.
No, we didn't perish that day.
But we did fall.
And though we're a bit battered,
a lot shattered,
by God, we're still here.
And slowly, oh so slowly,
we are rising once again.

— *Jennifer Fenwick, September 16, 2019*

IT'S THE SMALL THINGS

by Kim Mixon Hill

I've been strong after Hurricane Michael. I never really cried over it and only had one moment when I just felt tired and overwhelmed. It was after living at someone else's place for months, having to walk the dogs everywhere, and not being able to leave them. It was sleeping in someone else's bed knowing we had a lot of work ahead of us even after we were able to move back home. It was just the entirety of the situation because I've never been very adaptive of change. But, I took a selfie with very little makeup on, posted some "strong" hashtags, and carried on.

I stayed strong for months. In fact, I felt proud of myself for being so steadfast and not letting things warp my viewpoint. I celebrated places opening back up and always saw the bright side of everything that happened.

"Look, we have a new roof!"

"This restaurant is back open, let's go eat there!"

"The dogs have a new fenced in yard to play in."

"The stores are starting to open back up; I can't wait to go shopping."

"I've always wanted new windows in the house."

"This new shed holds way more than our others and we can always replace the stuff we lost.

And that was all great—until it wasn't. And it only took one small thing to topple the tower of my positivism.

It was one night while lying in bed. You know how your mind segues from one thought to another? So my thoughts took me to remembering when I worked at Sears a few years ago. My mom often went shopping by herself after my father died. She loved Sears since it was a mainstay in her life, having been around for decades. So, she was quite excited that I was working there.

I didn't work there for long, but that's irrelevant. I remember a couple of times she came to visit and see me while I was there.

My mom passed away a year or two after that and of course, she won't be coming to visit me anymore. But that's not what set me off since one had nothing to do with the other. It was thinking of how Sears is gone now. The whole mall is mostly gone.

I grew up with that mall. As a kid, we'd always visit certain stores like JC Penny and Sears. As a teen, I played on stage with my friends, being silly and making up dance moves to Prince. After high school, I worked at Gayfers (now Dillards) and spent lunch breaks at the food court. I've had dates there, met friends there, worked there, ate there, and shopped there.

While I didn't shop there often as I got older, maybe once in a while around Christmas, it's not there *for* me to shop. I was thinking of how I'd never be able to walk the floors again in the place where my mother came to visit me while I was working. I'll never be in the same store that she was so proud I was working at, regardless if I hated it or not. And that's all it took to start the waterworks.

I cried like I haven't in months. All the little things started adding up in a big way. While I still celebrate new beginnings and the path to recovery, I can't help but think that out of all the things I lost – one of them is as simple as browsing a store that my mother loved to visit. Hurricane Michael took that little thing away from me and it'll never be the same.

I'm still strong. I'm just a little weaker when I think of the mall. The one I didn't visit much, yet the one place I loathe to think of being gone forever. The place that will never have the echoes of our footprints again. The place that has so many memories for me. It's silly since so many people lost so much more. Many people would be happy if it was just the mall that was ruined. Maybe their homes would still be standing, and the mall would just be a minor inconvenience we all discussed and tried to remedy. But it's relevant to me and oddly, it's the one thing that made me finally cry.

Photo by Melinda JD Hall

RECONSTRUCTION

Reconstructing our lives.

Depending on teams.

Working together.

Living new dreams.

— Melinda JD Hall, June 18, 2019

THE PURPLE SKIES OF HURRICANE MICHAEL

by Deborah Hinton

Watercolor is a lot like life. There's always what you have in mind, and what you get. The secret is to find joy in what you get. — Deborah Hinton

I live in Panama City Beach, FL, which was recently hit hard by Hurricane Michael. My most recent series of watercolors is THE PURPLE SKIES OF HURRICANE MICHAEL, based on dramatic purple colors that appeared in the sky here after the storm.

The skies were caused by the strength of the storm scattering light rays to create unique purple colors. I was inspired by the beauty of these skies in the midst of the horrible devastation.

I have studied art at several schools, including the University of Cincinnati and Georgia Southern College. It is at these schools that I learned a lot of strict rules about painting, which I have been happily breaking ever since. I take a Taoist approach to my watercolors. I try to just "go with the flow." Instead of fighting to control the paint, I throw down some washes, and see how the paint surprises me. I always say that "sometimes the paint has a better idea than I do."

THE PURPLE SKIES OF HURRICANE MICHAEL

STUNNING PURPLE SKIES WERE SEEN IN THE HOURS AFTER HURRICANE MICHAEL DUE TO A RARE SCIENTIFIC PHENOMENON.

THE SCIENTIFIC EXPLANATION OF THE PURPLE SKIES INVOLVED A PHENOMENON CALLED SCATTERING. SCATTERING IS THE PROCESS BY WHICH PARTICLES IN THE AIR CHANGE THE DIRECTION IN WHICH LIGHT FROM THE SUN TRAVELS TO THE EARTH. HURRICANE MICHAEL WAS SO POWERFUL THAT THE MOISTURE IN THE AIR SCATTERED THE LIGHT RAYS, CAUSING THE AMAZING PURPLE SKIES.

To see these stunning images in color, visit gothsky.com. Photos by Deborah Hinton

YOUR SILENCE SPEAKS

You ask me what it's like
to live in such a strange world.
It wasn't like this before, I say.
Before that day. The one where
the winds raged ceaselessly,
roaring over and through
neighborhoods, communities,
miles and miles of our home.
Taking so much, leaving so little.
It wasn't like this before the
surging waters destroyed the
foundations. The ones that
supported our homes, our
livelihoods, our land.
In the span of a few hours,
the blink of an eye really,
our world was transformed.
From known to strange.
From comfort to chaos.
From before to this gut-wrenching after.
Yes.
Yes, we're grateful we survived.
But ok? No. This isn't normal.
This is wild and fluid.
Unchartered, unsettled.
Destruction so daunting.
This is heartbreaking and horrifying.
It's not the home we knew.
It'll never be that home again.
It's a saturating kind of pain.
A pain that lingers. And the world

outside? Outside our battered
borders? It moved on. In a day.
In a week. There was silence.
And we? We remained. Surrounded
by this vast brokenness.
Wearing our grief. Bearing the scars.
So many scars. Everywhere we look.
Everywhere we go, so changed and unfamiliar.
No. No, we are not ok.
You ask me what it's like to live in
such destruction.
When the world moves on, I say,
it's lonely. So very lonely.
Do you hear us? See us?
Are you listening?
It's your compassion we need.
Your honest and heartfelt awareness.
Your acknowledgment that we're
still here. That we matter. That we're
not alone. We thought nothing could
ever be worse, or more humbling,
than surviving that day. Living
in the aftermath? That, we can bare.
What's proven much harder,
what we never could have prepared for,
is your indifference.
And the message you convey
so loudly with your silence.

— *Jennifer N. Fenwick, March 7, 2019*

NOT ENOUGH BUCKETS

by Teri Elizabeth Hord

I remember October 7 like it was yesterday. My family and I get together every Sunday for "Family Day." All 12 of us. It was my turn to host lunch for us that day. We were all sitting out back listening to Eagle's Radio on Pandora when someone asked, "Hey, have y'all seen this tropical storm that's forming? They're saying it may hit here this week. Could end up being a Category 1 or 2 hurricane."

My heart sank for a brief moment.

I also had a voice in my head telling me not to over-react.

Again.

I felt fairly well prepared already. I had really worried about Irma the year before. Irma was the first major storm projected to make landfall here since my son was born over 4 and a half years ago. Preparing for a storm as a parent is much different than preparing for one before children.

We had plenty of water, canned goods, batteries, and a flashlight. I felt like that should be enough to get us through.

The following day, Steve went to work. I took Camden to school. It was a normal morning, coupled with a lingering sense of fear that kept looming in the back of my mind.

I told myself to not be ridiculous. It was just a tropical storm for God's sake.

As a precaution, I decided to fill up my gas tank and pick up some more water and non-perishables. We'd eat and drink them anyway, even if we didn't "need" them. There were several people who seemed to be preparing, but I wouldn't describe it as chaotic. It certainly was not like you would expect it to have been now that we've seen the outcome.

Camden's school informed me at pick-up they were closed until the storm passed for the staff and their families to make appropriate preparations.

That night, I begged Steve to take off work Tuesday. I couldn't imagine myself preparing for a hurricane alone with a four-year-old. Plus, it could get windy early and I couldn't have him on a roof in those conditions. I needed him home. We still needed to get our boat out of the water, bring all of our outdoor furniture inside, gather important documents, EVACUATE! No, that wasn't necessary.

I took a deep breath.

Photo by Teri Elizabeth Hord

At that time, Michael was still a Category 1, forecast to possibly become a Category 3.

My mind was fixated on Opal.

Opal wasn't Katrina. We're fine.

I Facebook messaged the owner of our house at the time Opal hit. He said we had one foot of water come inside. Ok, I can handle that. We have flood insurance and I hate the carpet in the master bedroom anyway.

But this could be a direct hit.

"More like Ivan in Pensacola?" I wondered.

I stayed up that night googling, "Hurricane Ivan images," "Hurricane Michael track," "Hurricane checklist," "Storm surge videos."

Steve was calm but woke me up around 4am. He said, "Hey, I had an idea. Google what time Home Depot opens."

"Why?"

"Just do it and see how much those 5-gallon buckets are."

Tuesday morning, shortly after we woke up, Michael had been upgraded to a Category 2.

I vividly remember Steve on the phone with a customer that morning pushing their appointment back from Wednesday to Thursday. "Tentatively, of course, until we know what this storm will do. Probably won't be a big deal. I'll keep you on the schedule. Call me if you have any questions."

He left to go to Home Depot.

He returned with fifty 5-gallon buckets.

"What the hell are those for? Bailing water out of the house?" I joked.

Just as he would read a grocery list, nonchalant and monotone, he said, "We're jacking everything up. I'm getting the drill to poke holes in all these, so they don't float away. We're really low, Teri. We will flood. We're gonna save what we can."

So, we got to work. We raised everything we had. Things from low cabinets went onto the countertops. We stacked furniture, one piece on top of the other, until it almost touched the ceiling. It was like a game of furniture Jenga. We made a "before" video for our inevitable insurance claim. Our neighbors got sandbags.

Photo by Teri Elizabeth Hord

I explained to my 4-year-old that our house would most likely fill with water, but we could live upstairs. It will be sad, but we will be ok. Camden caught a lizard outside and put it in one of the buckets. Inside the house. I didn't care.

That night, we settled in upstairs. We Face-Timed with our friends in Costa Rica and were in constant contact with our families, all in town, except my brother who decided to leave and stay with family in Alabama. They all begged us to come in town to stay with them. We were way too close to the coast they said. We would flood.

What if the surged reached upstairs? "Think about Camden!" my mom pleaded. I began to think they may be right.

I wouldn't say I begged, but I definitely strongly urged Steve to let us go in town to stay at my brother's. They'd gone to Alabama but wouldn't mind us staying there. It had to be safer than our house. Everyone knew it was better to be in town than on the beach. Do you not see the evacuation orders? Hello!

Steve said that was ridiculous. He'd inspected every one of their houses and watched the news and we were in the best place

I trusted him—The man who skydives and scuba dives and climbs on roofs for a living. A man who fears nothing

I trusted him

After the 10 o'clock news, I decided to take a "nap." I guess Steve dozed off sometime shortly after.

I went to bed that night on our mattress on the floor silently crying, wondering if we would end up like those poor people in Katrina reaching out for helicopters to rescue them off the tops of their flooded homes. I actually considered going to get the pool floats out of our garage. Ridiculous, I know.

I was terrified.

At 4am, we were jolted awake by that horribly shrill sound they use for Amber alerts coming from our cell phones. This would be the first of many in the coming days. How they could send 50 of those annoying alerts to your phone per day, yet no one had cell service for miles, remains a mystery to me. Groggy and sore, our hearts now pounding, we turned the television on. At 4am Wednesday, just 8 hours before Hurricane Michael made landfall, it had finally reached Category 4 status.

I will never forget looking at Steve, my eyes filling with tears, asking, "What should we do now?

I knew what he would say. "We're fine." "Stop over-reacting." "Calm down."

But he didn't.

Instead, he looked me dead in the eyes and very calmly, but very seriously said, "We need to leave. Pack a suitcase. We don't have much time."

It was an out of body experience.

I began quickly, but methodically packing for what I just knew would be all we had left after the next 8 hours passed. I stayed oddly calm until I called my mom to let her know our plans. We both cried. I was scared. Actually, there, in that very moment, I was the most scared I'd ever been in my entire life.

We had no idea where we were going. We just knew we were going west.

When I got into the car, the outer rain bands were already upon us. I glanced back and saw Steve standing in the doorway just looking at our house. I knew what he was doing. He was saying goodbye. It broke my heart. We didn't know if we could make it over the bridge or if it would be closed due to the ever-increasing wind. There was a fairly good possibly we'd be forced to ride out the storm in the car. At that point, I didn't care. That seemed like a better option than remaining in our home.

I called every hotel and motel beginning in Destin and working my way west. I got an alert on the way that the winds had reached a staggering 155mph. Sustained. I will forever have ingrained in my mind the look Steve had on his face when I told him that. It was like he saw the future and knew what was coming. It still gives me chills to think about it.

"We don't build houses this way," he said, and kept driving.

We finally ended up in Mobile in a musty motel room in a bad part of town. We watched the storm hit from that muggy, dirty room, not having a clue what we'd come back to, if anything. Of course the cell towers went down fairly early. We had lost communication with the inside world.

We woke up before dawn the next day, not that we really slept, and headed back east. I remember reaching Pier Park and wondering why there seemed to be no damage. Maybe it wasn't as bad as we'd thought. But how? No, that couldn't be right.

Then we reached Thomas Drive.

We dodged power lines and downed trees. We came home to a world no one could have prepared us for. Our once beautifully manicured neighborhood was now a gigantic mess of twisted, broken, mangled trees. There was debris everywhere. People were missing parts of their roofs. Cars were in ditches. We cried. The sun was out. "How ironic," I thought.

I was confused. We had prepared to flood.

We parked our car down the street. The roads were blocked with giant fallen pine trees. With a four-year-old and a dog, we finally made it home.

The relief I felt at that moment was indescribable. Our house was a mess, don't get me wrong. Our roof was missing several shingles. We lost 8 trees. Our brand new pavered driveway was torn up pretty bad. Outside lights were broken and missing. Our pool pump and fence were broken due to fallen trees. We had, what I now know to be, about $100,000 worth of damage. But I didn't care. All of that was trivial. I had expected to come home to a house that had three feet of water inside. I think, in that moment, I actually laughed like a wild, crazed person experiencing a manic episode. But inside, I knew there was nothing funny about any of this.

We made the trek back to our car, now scratched on both sides from maneuvering through the debris. We went to check on the rest of our family in town.

Unfortunately, they hadn't fared as well. I will always remember pulling up to my brother's house. His yard was covered in insulation, like it had just survived a blizzard of melt-proof snow. Most of his roof was on the ground in the neighbor's yard. And the smell. You could smell it before you even went inside. Mold.

My eyes filled with tears. I looked at Steve and squeezed his hand, silently thanking him for not letting me have my way and ride the storm out here. I was thankful my brother didn't either.

He is still living in a travel trailer.

Later that day, we drove to Lynn Haven to check on Steve's parents. Everywhere we looked was total destruction. We drove to Parker to check on our old neighbors and old house the next day. I don't have words for that. Most of the homes on that street will be torn down.

"How could this be? How is this possible?" I kept asking over and over.

We had prepared to flood.

We had prepared for town to be safe.

We had prepared for the entire beach to be destroyed.

We hadn't prepared for this.

There were not enough buckets at Home Depot to have saved us from Michael.

And I often wonder, "What ever happened to that lizard?"

DEBRIS

by Heather Parker

February 10, 2019—My brain spins when I hear that the City of Panama City has picked up—the people of Panama City have tossed out—3,200,000 cubic yards of debris in the 4 months since the hurricane. A normal year is roughly 100,000 cubic yards—32 years' worth of 'debris' have been thrown out.

But that word. Debris. Excluding the occasional tragedy, I think of most debris as being trash by choice, like—It broke, you tossed it out, along with the packaging the new one came in. Debris.

You decided to trim your trees and replace your old landscape timbers. Or you saved some money, invested in a new front door and porch railings. Tree trimmings and old wood—debris.

A kid grew out of their car seat, old one is too bad to donate, it becomes debris.

That's debris. Empty, meaningless debris. You're done with it, no one else needs it. Toss it out.

But this? This hurricane damage and destruction? It's not yard debris and old building materials and used up furniture. It's more. It's more than just debris.

It's people's sheds and workshops. Where they protected their belongings from the weather and from thieves. It's their lawnmowers and bicycles and camping gear and summer patio decorations, and their hobbies and crafts. It's their lifestyles.

It's chunks of sidewalk, sidewalk that we used to walk to the neighbor's house; it's fences and street signs, bushes and vines, barking backyard dogs and frolicking squirrels. It's flowers and yard decorations. It's curb appeal and landscaping. It's function and beauty. Personality and charm. Identity and place.

31 million cubic yards of debris left by Hurricane Michael has been removed since the storm hit in October 2018. Photo by Lisa Parsons/Shutterstock

It's mangled front and back yards, with gaping holes from ripped up trees. It's twisted ankles and nails in tires and feet, and parking ruts and torn up roads. It's crushed cars and damaged suspension and broken lights.

It's people's trees. The town's trees. The earth's trees. It was the canopy of protection, it shielded the ugliness of this town, it shaded us and our dogs from the sun. The trees held the water, so our yards and roads didn't flood. Homes to squirrels and birds. Air cleaners. Warnings of storms on the way. Protectors. Guardians. Trees.

It's our windows and doors and front porches. It's protection and sunlight and beautiful curtains and door knockers and peep holes and rocking chairs and lemonade on a hot summer day.

It's our ceilings, in matted pasty chunks smashed onto great grandmother's dresser. It's the rest of the ceiling, smashed into the carpet you spent hours choosing last year when you got a raise. It's the ceiling, that kept the attic crap in the attic and not on your floor where the cat can eat it.

It's our walls. The walls to our homes. What separates inside from outside, hot and cold, wet and dry, safe and not safe.

It's our box of photos, the ones we've collected and meant to scan into the computer. It's our computer, where we write poetry and save recipes, plan our future and balance our budgets.

It's our clothes. What we wear to work and out for anniversary dinner, and on vacation, and to snuggle in bed.

It's our beds. Where we sleep. And dream. And love.

It's our personal history. The history of us, the history of our family. Our children's toys. Our husband's collection of rare books. Our cherished holiday decorations. The furniture we bought together.

It's our greater history. The history of our town. Our historic buildings. Our statement of the past, our look towards the future. Our neighbors homes. The old country store that will someday be recreated to look old and it'll be a fake imposter and we'll have to accept it.

It's our present. It's a loss of authenticity. Loss of the way things were. It's vacant corners and dust, dirt and sand swirls in the wind. It's new sound patterns and the baby can't nap because the afternoon sun comes in the new window and the new cheap crib has to be moved to another place in the room.

It's 'what used to be there?' And facing the reality of how quickly we can forget what we don't see every day. It's wanting to remember, and knowing you can't, you shouldn't, you have to move on. It's spending money you don't have, to buy back your security and protection, your walls and doors and roof and knowing, accepting, you can't buy back what you had.

It's shingles. Everyday. Another shingle. And as you put that shingle in the pile next to the can on the curb, you know—someone's getting wet, crying, filling a drip bucket, cold, hot, paying extra on their electric bill, still trying to get a hot water heater and a plumber and a drywall installer, arguing with the roofer, fighting with their spouse, pleading with the insurance company, while fixing dinner for their children in the microwave because the stove got ruined, and wondering if that sound at the makeshift plywood door is your dog returning because he ran away three days ago because you have no fence, and you can't see very well because there is no outside light anymore because it's debris.

It's the void we look at every day, swallowing us up piece by piece, bit by bit.

It's the acknowledgment that we will never be the same again. Inside and outside. We'll never have what we had again. We'll never again be what we were.

It's force. The force of the wind. Being forced to change before you've grieved. Force of movement. Force of nature. Forcefully new and forcefully there, at every moment.

It's not debris. It's everything. It's everything we don't have any more in our splintered selves, in our broken homes, and in our empty town.

These are the things the rest of the world doesn't hear. These are the things we didn't hear when it wasn't us. And we get to live with that, craft our lives in it, raise our children with it, and rebuild our town without it. This debris. It's everything.

ESCAPE

We understand.

The need for escape.

The desire to move on,

As though all is well.

But we can't, you see.

We, who lived through that day.

The reminders are all around us.

We see them at every turn.

It's in the barren limbs,

of the trees left standing.

In the broken remains,

of the structures left crumbling.

In the weary eyes,

of the souls left struggling.

On every corner.

We see the aftermath.

The war-torn remnants.

The ever-present reminders.

We understand.

But for us, escape is not an option.

This is our home.

This storm ravaged landscape.

We cannot turn away.

Cannot unsee the destruction.

Cannot unhear the raging winds.

Cannot unfeel the fear.

We remember. All that was.

We grieve. All that's lost.

We long. Oh, how we long.

For rest. For healing.

For our determination to be enough.

We understand. And we pray.

How fervently we pray.

For ourselves. And for you.

That you never have to live,

through a hell like this one.

— Jennifer N. Fenwick, June 12, 2019

Photo by Jan Prewett

MICHAEL'S ANGELS

by Tracy Johnstone

It all started with a Facebook post on January 18, 2019. What we would call 100 days after the storm. All time is now measured in before and after the storm. I suspect that will be true for quite some time.

The post read, "I feel like I want to talk to all the ladies out there for a minute. Following Hurricane Katrina in New Orleans a group of hometown ladies gathered themselves and created *Women of the Storm*. I'm curious if there's such a group in Panama City who can be our voice of destruction, our voice of despair, and our voice of determination to spread the news about our calamities to those who can help improve our recovery but are just unaware of what it's really like here. If there's even just a few of you who are willing to be the voices of our community to the outside, I'll open up my office and y'all can figure out your message, who you want to tell, and how you want to tell it. Ladies, are you interested?"

The post read like a gospel invitation. An invitation to step forward; to take a step away from the chaos of recovery. This was a salvation call for each of us as women and for the community that we all call home.

You see we were 100 days into a recovery from a category five hurricane that ravaged our town—wiping out over 80 percent of our tree canopy, demolishing 1 in 10 homes, and destroying nearly every church building we had. We were naked. We were weary and exposed. But mostly, we were finding hope just plain hard to come by.

So, we gathered together as "sisters of the storm" to figure out exactly who we were. We knew we had been forgotten by the media, corporate America, and it would seem by our own country. We knew we had to do something to change that. We were as grassroots as it gets. No structure, no budget, no agenda; and therein lay the magic, the hope, the sisterhood that would become *Michel's Angels.*

Local attorney and civic leader, William Harrison, opened his law offices for the initial meeting From that meeting, Michael's Angels was born. Photo by Tracy Johnstone.

We did what mothers and grandmothers have done for centuries; we told the story. We became the storytellers of Hurricane Michael and all things recovery. We became educated in the legislative process and rallied the cry of despair. It has been how many days since the storm and still no state or federal funding? We made sure our stories were told and our voices were heard.

The Rally in Tally, organized by Michael's Angels, brought much needed focus to the plight of the survivors of Michael. Photo by Tracy Johnstone.

The people of the panhandle were battered by this storm, you could feel the desperation in the air. The debris piles taller than my home were dwindling while the anxiety of insolvent municipalities and depleted budgets escalated. Our self-rescue efforts could only take us so far.

So, we gathered our villages and we took our story to the steps of the capital and opened the *Book of Michael* for all the world to see. It was the *Rally in Tally* that not only got the attention of the press, but it was a movement of solidarity for our community that was a balm for our many wounds.

This sisterhood of the storm called *Michael's Angels* took on a life of its own and took over much of our spare time too. Have you ever been to a meeting and been one of the folks to hang around and talk, clean up, wrap things up? If so, then you know that hanging around to help makes you a helper, which makes you a volunteer, which makes you one of those privileged souls in this case to do the behind the scenes work.

We were all still in that "I don't need another thing on my plate" phase. Displaced from homes, trying to get a business back open and functional, contractors, insurance people, all while keeping our own sanity post storm. I believe we did not pick *Michael's Angels*, *Michael's Angels* picked us.

Dr. Shane Collins, local radio personality, joins the ladies of Michael's Angels at Rally in Tally in April 2019. Photo by Tracy Johnstone.

It was finally the perfect storm of women to fight the storm that ravaged our community. The business owner, the medical professionals, the mothers, the PhD candidate, the political guru, the school administrator, the wife, and the attorney. And we met. And we planned. We made the phone calls, sent the emails, wrote the briefings, went to the meetings, and rallied with the people of this amazing community.

So, what happened next? When the storyteller is good every good listener wants to know!

The satisfaction of work well done, minds changed, bills passed, offenses forgiven, had given rise like yeast to bread of an undeniable, unquestionable, unending sisterhood of the storm between the six of us.

The name *Michael's Angels* and our work may be archived but friendships and bonds we have formed are stronger than those winds at the eye of the storm.

Photo by Tracy Johnstone.

◆　◆　◆

8 MONTHS

8 months.

Some people have repairs.

Some people are waiting.

Some people scattered everywhere.

8 months.

Blue roof sea.

Contractors, equipment, supplies.

We miss our trees.

8 months.

How are you coping?

Lives still a mess.

Sitting here hoping.

8 months.

Masters of policy.

Breaking American Dream promises.

We just want back life's quality.

8 months.

— *Melinda JD Hall, June 1, 2019*

CHATAUQUA

by Cynthia McCauley

Chautauqua is an Iroquois word meaning, 'working together.' Founded on the premise of learning by working together in service to others, *Chautauqua Learn and Serve Charter School* strives to emulate, on a pocket-sized scale, our distinguished parent organization, the *Chautauqua Institution* near Buffalo, NY.

Entering the gates of the Chautauqua Institution one recognizes immediately a parallel universe. Its ideals were planted and nurtured in the Utopian Era and continue to grow. The Institution envelops your senses with a shared commitment to 'inspire the best of human values.' This, too, is our lofty goal. Perhaps laughable, given we are a tiny facility attended by young adults with disabilities, but walking up the driveway of our Chautauqua on a school day, surrounded by the sublime art of *Heather Parker*, many beautiful flowers, and the smiles and spirit of the Chautauqua students and their gifted Bay High School mentors, a sense of righteous purpose elevates all. It is both a place and an inspiration.

On October 11 2018, cutting a narrow way out the back door of our home with edge clippers, my husband, Carroll, and I finally made it through the tree fallen forest of our driveway to the street. The scene was apocalyptic. Lucky enough to have cellphone carriers with service, Carroll and I took separate paths and made a way to our work. He went to his office; I worked my way to school. Usually it's a 30-minute walk. This day it took three hours. Gasps, fear, and panic filled the time. The city was devastated. Brick building were crumbling. Could anything be left of our little wooden schoolhouse? And, if not?

Turning off 11th Street to Magnolia Avenue my heart was pounding. I could see in the distance the metal awning over the deck curled to ribbons. Closer, I saw most shingles gone from the roof. A large tree impaled the plate glass window of the front porch. Through the tangle of trees and branches I noticed a door dangling in the breeze.

Arriving at the house that serves as Chautauqua Learn and Serve Charter School 's main building the day after Michael, director, Cynthia McCauley, was greeted with utter chaos and destruction. Photo by Cynthia McCauley.

I struggled to get to the double-doors of a classroom opening onto the deck. Always locked at night by a dead bolt, these French doors were somehow separated. The bottom hinge was ripped from the doorframe. The top hinge held. Through this flapping door I entered the school.

The painted tongue and groove ceilings were buckled and dripping. Torrential rains of Hurricane Michael puddled across the old plank floors. Rain filled the caldron shaped punch bowl, the orange plastic Jack-O-Lantern chip bowls, and the giant silver metal tub for apple bobbing, decorations in waiting for our annual Halloween Party; just another bright spot in the lives of our disabled students stolen by Hurricane Michael.

Mustering all the agility and nimbleness a senior citizen can deploy, I made my way over, under, around and through the massive snarl of trees, branches, metal, trash, shingles, boards, and more to survey the small campus.

The deck, the ramps, the railings, the gazebo, the fence, the power poles, the greenhouse, the storage shed—everything was ripped apart by wind or crushed by more trees than I knew were there. The good news was obvious, the schoolhouse and two of the three portable classrooms were—damaged, but standing! With some work, we could continue.

In black garbage bags I dragged the dripping tubs of ice cream and party-ready packs of hot dogs from the freezer to the curb, making myself first do the job I had to do. Next, I did the job I was anxious to do; I contacted the staff. I just wanted to ask them to come to school when they could. We would 'get started!' Sending a group text had the feel of putting a group message in a bottle and sending it out to sea. Who had cell service? Who had power to charge their phone? Who could get out of their driveway? Who was even in town?

My phone started ringing with some answers. The next day Carissa came smiling up the school driveway, then Jimmy, and then Heather.

Heather started contacting students with her cellphone and making a spreadsheet the old-fashioned way-a yellow pad and a ruler. Carissa was scrubbing the floors with bleach, and Jimmy was picking through the railing trying to salvage any usable pieces when an unknown van pulled up. It was so loaded down; the wheels weren't visible. It was my son-in-law, Chuck, with a van load of supplies from the *Sunrise Rotary Club of Lafayette, Indiana*. In no time, he had an industrial folding ladder and giant blue tarps next to the house. He headed for the roof.

So early in the post—hurricane process, he had to use his persecutor's badge to enter Bay County. As for me, I sent messages to the boards of both our programs and started looking for roofers and debris haulers. We wanted to be the first school up and running. It was starting to feel like we could.

With no running water or electricity, we sustained ourselves with the bottles of water and graham crackers we keep for the needy when we hand out trolley tokens.

Then one day we heard a loudspeaker. It was the Red Cross. Of all the work Chautauqua proudly does for the needy, this was our first experience on the other side of the equation. It was wonderful and humbling. We each walked away with tears in our eyes as we carried our plates of food.

While no one called them to come work, slowly our students started showing up to help. There is nothing more therapeutic than talking about your storm experiences and, as our name states, "working together."

Four days before we were about to reopen for the school year, most of our students and all the staff were there and working hard—Heather Parker, our artist, called to see if we needed any volunteer help. We said, 'signs, signs of cheer.' This she did with her usual skill.

We officially opened school November 7th, but we were all there November 5th. Staff held signs, 'We are Family,' 'Find something that makes you happy and use it to make others happy,' and more. Two panels of plywood fill the space of the plate glass window with,

"Can't Control It Chautauqua, Roll with It." The facility was pasted, duck taped, and nailed together with love—and it held.

Amid the damage, and it was extensive, it escapes no one that the images that inspire us were totally untouched—the giant murals of the grand places of the Chautauqua Institution. The *Hall of Philosophy* where ideas are presented, *Bestor Plaza* where ideas are discussed, and *Chautauqua Park* where new knowledge is processed with the evening sunset, these murals had not a scratch. Even the mural of the *Miller Bell Tower*, a symbol of 'knowledge for all,' stood with remarkable presence as the portable to which it was attached was smashed by a tree. *Chautauqua Learn and Serve School* is truly both a place and an inspiration.

'*Learning by working together in service to others*' was and is leading us through this trauma. There is much need for our service to others in the community. As we volunteer in numerous places across the county and the world, the disabled and gifted working to together, we are, as our lofty goal requires, "inspiring the best of human values."

The school's inspiring murals lovingly painted by local artist, Heather Parker, remained totally untouched. Photo by Cynthia McCauley

REMINDERS

In the middle of the raging storm,

My eyes glanced up and light took form.

A prism painted in radiant hue,

Against a sky of breaking blue.

A reminder that,

these storms won't last.

As life reveals,

This too shall pass.

— Jennifer N. Fenwick, July 11, 2019

Photo by Laura McManus

BACK IN BUSINESS

by Teri Elizabeth Hord

"Mommy, Mommy! They're back! They're back!" A little voice and excited footsteps raced down the hall toward my bedroom.

I opened my eyes, only half able to see, and glanced at the clock. 5:39am.

"Great," I thought to myself.

I still had six minutes until my alarm would go off.

"Couldn't this have waited?"

I rolled over and mustered up the energy respond. "What's back, baby?"

"The geckos, Mom! They're back. I got one!"

My five-year-old excitedly brought his prized reptile over to show me. I looked at my husband, who had followed our son into our room, and for a brief moment, we made eye contact. A feeling of peace and relief washed over me.

"They *are* back, huh? Look at that. He's adorable," I smiled.

Every summer we are plagued with a gecko invasion inside of our home. I can't tell you how they get in, but they just do. I'm not much for reptiles, so it helps that I live with 3 males. For the last two years, I have spent the summer googling how to get rid of these wretched creatures. Eggshells, garlic, the whole bit. Nothing ever works. Get rid of one, get two in its place.

But this year, they never came.

They never came and strangely, I missed them.

I missed them like I miss the mall. And Tranquility Blue. And Uncle Ernie's.

I missed them like I miss Boar's Head. And Waterworx. And Pelican's.

I missed them almost as much as I miss the trees.

I missed them because they were part of my old life. My old, ordinary, normal life.

Well, what was my life before the storm.

I expected them to show up this summer. But they never came. Just one more missing piece to our life puzzle.

But today, they came, and we welcomed them with open arms.

"We're back in business!" Camden declared.

"Yes, we are, honey. We sure are."

Photo by Teri Elizabeth Hord

I NEVER KNEW

I never knew when we went to bed 10/9/18
that would be the last time we would ever sleep in our bed.
I never knew that on 10/10/2018—6 months ago today—our
Home and belongings would be gone.
I never knew that we would be hit by a storm and that day
would forever change our lives.
I never knew a lot of my neighbors, but we quickly came to
know them and work as a team helping each other.
I never knew how long we could actually go without eating or
drinking—we just forgot.
I never knew how broken I could feel losing my wedding dress,
veil, and wedding albums.
I never knew how at times I really didn't want to go on
but forced myself to anyway.
But I do know we are survivors,
and we will come back stronger than ever.
I do know I will never take anything for granted.
Things can change in the blink of an eye.
I do know my husband and I have laughed more in the past 6
months than we have in the past 35 years.
I do know that we are 850 strong and we are stronger than ever
here in the Panhandle.
I do know that God had His hand on us here,
and for that I will always Praise His Holy name.

— Jane Smith, April 10, 2019

The scarred landscape and bare, broken trees will take years to rehabilitate following Michael.
Photo by Joseph Thomas Photography/Shutterstock

MELANCHOLY

by Erica McNabb Floyd

Melancholy. That's an honest description of where I am. I've had good days and sad days over the last 10 months.

But a couple days ago while having a heart to heart with my 13-year-old daughter, a knife pierced my heart. She was visibly sad and disturbed.

I had asked her to take the cat litter to the garbage can Sunday evening. Upon coming back in the house I noticed she had changed. I asked what was wrong and she began to weep as she spoke. She said the smell of the garbage took her back.

I didn't think our garbage was rancid enough to make her cry and failed to see her point at first. As she explained, in the days following Hurricane Michael, she went for a walk through our neighborhood. In her mind, the smell of everyone's refrigerator contents rotting in the hot temperatures, had a different smell. At that time she thought it was the smell of dead bodies, people who had died and had not had their bodies recovered. She found herself alone in what, to her, felt like a war zone in that moment. We obviously know now it wasn't the smell of bodies decaying but she didn't know that then.

I had never been told this. I had no idea that for the past 10 months my daughter had carried this burden of associating the smell of garbage with the aftermath of the storm. I didn't realize PTSD could be brought on by a common smell.

In my defense, I clean my fridge out Sunday mornings after church as our pickup is on Mondays. So by Sunday evening when she takes out the cat litter it has a bit of a stench.

I have been unintentionally making my daughter relive that fearful moment every week for months.

So I will carry this sadness and burden for her from now on. I will carry the litter to the can on Sunday evenings, so she doesn't relive that moment.

But now I will relive it through her account when I smell garbage and have to fight tears of my own.

AUTHOR'S NOTE: *The sudden and overwhelming nature of natural disasters can lead to the development of Post-Traumatic Stress Syndrome (PTSD). If you notice PTSD symptoms in yourself or a loved one, experts encourage you to seek a health care professional.*

CRACKS

His demons are back

They were with him before the storm

But he used to hide them in the trees

Now that's not an option

She yelled at some rubble today

Not sure why she did it

Maybe because that spot had been cleared

Guess that building was not done purging

He sits in his car outside the office

Trying to get up the nerve to face the day

He's handling the big stuff

But a small thing might make him crack

She has no passion for the things

that used to make her whole

Is this just the way it is now?

She's not willing to consider that

— *Jason Hedden, March 12, 2019*

Photo by Jason Hedden

6500 MILES AWAY

by Shaun Mulligan

My wife Wanda and I were anticipating our first cruise that would take us to Rome, Greece and Israel on October 4, 2018. It was a cool morning when my wife's cousin Linda was to transport us to the airport from my wife's parents dream home that we had just moved into after major renovation.

As we drove up through Lynn Haven and to HWY 77 never would I realize that the scenery would change from the tall pines lining the highway. Upon arriving at the Panama City Beach Airport, we met five traveling companions from our church for a Land of the Bibles cruise.

After spending two days in Rome seeing the local sights we departed on October 7th from Italy to Crete. I had been checking my phone and saw some posts on Facebook about a tropical depression off the west coast of Cuba that was tracking north to the Gulf Coast region.

After spending about 4 hours on the island of Crete our group departed on October 10th to our next destination, Jerusalem, Israel. On the ship we had one news station from the United States and that was Fox News. We turned on the TV in our cabin at 9 PM (8 hours ahead) and watched with disbelief as Hurricane Michael approached our hometown of Panama City, Florida.

The next morning as the sun rose off the port in Israel, we woke up to the news that the Hurricane was more devastating than anyone could have predicted. The others in our group were receiving photos and bits of information from family members of the aftermath. Two days later I received a text message with photos of our home that had lost about one third of the roof and sustained severe wind and water damage inside.

The remaining ten days on the cruise were surreal. The seven of us from Panama City were so far away and the only thing we could do was pray and comfort each other as we would be arriving back home to a different world.

The last few days on the cruise ship I received a phone call from a field adjuster requesting that I meet me at my home in a couple of days. I explained that I would be happy to meet with him after I arrived home. I also had to deal with having a tarp placed on the home to prevent any further water damage while we were away.

After flying back to Charlotte, NC and renting a car to Panama City we arrived home on Oct 25th. Arriving that afternoon we entered the Bay County Line on HWY 231. Seeing our home for the first time, the devastation was horrific. Pictures cannot adequately convey the emotions of what we're seeing.

The days and weeks trying to assimilate to this new way of life was a struggle for everyone.

My wife and I decided, after much thought, to take some time to settle before undertaking the arduous task of rebuilding. There were so many others distress and need and not enough contractors to go around.

We had small block home on our property that went on the market before we departed for our cruise. This home became our new home while we worked out the details with our insurance company. We had just renovated our home 6-months prior to Michael. Rebuilding it would take far longer.

After consulting with two different contractors it was concluded that our home was beyond 50% damaged and that we had two choices. First, we could gut the home to the studs and bring everything up to code in the home, originally built in 1974. Second, we could demo the home and rebuild entirely. The cost and time for both options was the same.

We chose to demolish and rebuild. We sold our new kitchen appliances and gave our counter tops and the cabinets that were not water damaged to some friends so they could rebuild their home after the Michael.

In early May 2019, we offered the interior doors to a woman from our church whose home was located in the Parker area and was severely damaged.

A retired contractor and friend of ours was able to remove and salvage the rafters and trusses of our home, along with the 2x4's, flooring, windows, and other fixtures to help others whose homes had suffered damage and who had little or no insurance to cover the costs to rebuild.

For three months, with just three of us working from early morning to noon each day, we disassembled our former home piece by piece. The lumber and materials we were able to salvage went to five homes that needed repair that would otherwise not have been financially possible for the owners.

Being able to assist others, rather than focusing on our own losses, has helped Wanda and tremendously through this experience.

On a personal note, we've met with a local contractor and have decided to build a smaller home. Hopefully, construction will begin by the end of 2019.

Each disaster becomes a steppingstone for growth.

— *ERIN BROCKOVICH*

THE FORGOTTEN COAST

by Jennifer N. Fenwick

Since October 10, 2018, counties impacted by Hurricane Michael, are suffering. Loss of jobs and income, along with closed and damaged schools, a housing crisis, and increasing uncertainty coupled have coalesced into a perfect storm of their own.

August 31, 2019—As I look around the barren landscape and notice the still clinging blue tarps, the vacant lots where homes and businesses used to stand, the stark and revealing evidence that some forgotten disaster occurred here, I have to wonder, exactly when the rest of the world decided Michael was nothing more than a blip on their radar?

For us, Category 5, Hurricane Michael changed everything. Just ten months ago we were struggling through the first days and weeks following the destruction he left behind.

Those of us who have lived in the aftermath of Michael have weathered countless storms since that day last October. Though progress is being made, the region and its people are suffering. Yet, the world outside has largely forgotten us.

A recent survey conducted by *Rebuild 850*, an initiative launched shortly after the storm to advocate on behalf of hurricane victims still trying to rebuild their lives, showed nearly half of respondents would do nothing to help people affected by Michael and nearly 75 percent said they would not consider donating money to help with relief efforts (*FLAPOL*, 26 JUN 2019).

For those outside the region, who mistakenly believe that all is well, the numbers don't lie, though they are rarely, if ever reported on.

Hurricane Michael was the first Category 5 storm to hit the United States since Hurricane Andrew, tearing a path through some of the poorest parts of Florida. Insurers report nearly $7 billion in losses across nearly 150,000 claims that have been filed (*Tampa Bay Times*, 26 AUG 2019).

In Mexico Beach, where Michael's eye passed, virtually obliterating the tiny coastal community, the losses are staggering, and rebuilding is slow.

Eighty percent of Mexico Beach, FL, was destroyed by Michael.
Image by Alan Strourgeon/Shutterstock

The city's budget depends on property taxes. But 70 percent of the storm's 27,000 homes were damaged or completely destroyed by the storm. Before the storm about 1,1000 people lived in Mexico Beach. Now only 400 or so remain. The city doesn't currently have a gas station or a grocery store (*mypanhandle.com*, 18 AUG 2019).

Residents throughout the entire Panhandle region continue to struggle with the aftereffects of Michael. The emotional trauma of living through a natural disaster of this magnitude and scope have left many in a perpetual state of fear and anxiety.

With the start of the 2019 Hurricane Season, many residents are still living in tents or ruined homes, waiting for contractors or government funds to help them rebuild. Some fear heavier rains attracting black mold, with roofs still covered by tarps that can leak, even with a typical summer's afternoon thunderstorm. Others are wary about water damage from flooding, as state and municipalities still work to clear debris, or about weakened trees from Michael that might topple in a lesser storm (*Miami Herald*, 10 JUL 2019).

In Bay County too, progress is slow, and the aftereffects of Michael are still readily visible. Debris and damaged buildings remain along Highway 98, the main drag, and 5,000 kids are still considered "homeless," crashing with friends and family or living in FEMA tents and trailers. About 30 percent of the school kids never came back. More than 50 percent of the apartments still are not liveable (*Fox News*, 31 MAY 2019).

The sad truth is, that outside of the impacted areas, the rest of the country is oblivious to the continued hardships survivors of Michael face.

We recognize that we are not the only region of the country to suffer from natural disasters. All we ask is please, just please don't minimize our struggles or trivialize our survival by continuing to overlook Michael's destruction and impact. The forgotten coast we may be, but rest assured, not a single one of us who lived through that day, who continue to exist in the aftermath, will ever forget.

How can we? The destruction is still all around us.

Remnants of the destruction unleashed by Hurricane Michael are still plainly visible throughout the Panhandle, even ten months later. Image by Terry Kelly/Shutterstock

◆ ◆ ◆

RELUCTANT TO POST

We're much better off than most
That's why I'm reluctant to post
We're blessed to have another place to stay.
Sadly, it's so far away.
We were spared the first-hand experience of Michael.
But returned three days later
to experience the devastation of it all.
Our house took a hit, but it's intact.
We have the greatest neighbors
and church family, that's a fact.
We brought supplies, a generator
and an AT&T phone early on.
Our neighbors and church family
were our chief concern.
Debris was removed from our yard.
That was the easy part,
the rest is going to be hard.
Waiting patiently for our turn for repairs to begin.
After four months our roof was dried in;
still waiting on the tin.
Pack out, tear out, dry out, all new terms for us.
Shy of five months, when will it start,
we ask as we lose trust.
We can't live in our house;

how many phones calls before you're a pest?
Whether this contractor, that contractor,
Insurance company and all the rest?
We're reluctant to ask neighbors to do anything else.
Guilt tells us we should be there and do it ourselves.
So what should we do?
 Stay in a motel close by and twiddle our thumbs?
Until there is something that requires our presence?
That seems dumb.
Still we know we're better off than most.
That's why I'm reluctant to post.

AUTHOR'S NOTE: I received this beautiful piece from a gentleman who reached out to me through my Facebook page. He asked me to post this on his behalf but wanted to remain anonymous. I decided to include it here because even all these months later, it still speaks to me. Anonymous survivor, you may be reluctant to post, but I am honored to do so

◆ ◆ ◆

THE DAY MY WORLD BLEW AWAY

It rained,
It blew,
I prayed anew,
To be saved or taken away.
Three hours of terror,
That seemed like days,
My prayers were answered,
He took me away.
To a place I never imagined,
Vaguely familiar but not.
Silence reigned and darkness fell,
The only sounds distant alarms
And approaching helicopters—

Dawn is coming,
A brand-new day,
Red marks on the doorways,
To prove we're not dead.
He passes us over,
And now we know why.
We'll make it better,
In our own special way.
It will take years to accomplish,
Teamwork and dedication.

The story still to be written,
Our rebirth and regeneration.

We live with hope
And fight despair.
Where is our help?
It's in the air—
The needs are great,
The cost is greater.
So many months later,
And it's still a crater.

We make our plans,
Not all is lost.
The only barrier,
Is the cost—
For those outside,
It's easy to forget,
Our needs are still large,
So many still unmet—

Please don't forget us,
Like some have 911.
Someday we'll be accountable,
When we meet in heaven.

—Lisa J. Munson, *July 23, 2019*

WET SLIPPERS

by Heather Parker

My life is like a post hurricane version of "There's a hole in my bucket, dear Liza, dear Liza!" playing on repeat.

"Why are my wet slippers on the table in the front room?"

Because I washed them but had to take them out of the dryer before it was done.

Because I had to flip the breaker.

Because the light bulb exploded.

"Where are my pliers so I can unscrew the rest of the broken lightbulb?"

Out the side door on the ledge because I was trying to pull a nail out of a board so I could plug up the hole in the ceiling.

But you can't go that way. I just put polyurethane on that part of the floor, you can't walk there.

Which is why I had to wash your slippers because I couldn't get the dog to go out the other door because that's not the way she goes, and she peed on your slippers. You'll have to go around front to get to the side.

"I'll need the work light to go around front, so I don't fall in the trench the guy dug to replace the water line. You know, the one that we thought would solve all our water pressure problems but didn't."

Can't, the last battery is dead. I used up the other ones doing the floor and hunting around in the attic for the mouse that got in because the roofer didn't come when he said he'd come to fix the soffit. And I couldn't charge any because I had to flip the breaker because the lightbulb exploded.

"So is there more broken glass in the bathroom?"

Probably, and the shop vac is in there, you'll have to sidestep around it in the dark. Better wear your slippers.

Heather Parker is a local artist and creative director at Floriopolis. Since Hurricane Michael she has been the creative force behind the Great Create, which was held in April and Art Break Day held in September. Both events encouraged healing through the arts and will be held again next year.

Heather's beautiful artwork can be seen in various locations around town, most notably at Chautauqua Learn and Serve School. She and her daughter, Megan, painted the stunning murals decorating the school's 56' fence.

A NEED TO PAINT

I need to paint.
If I don't paint, I forget to see.
How the light shines through the window,
the shapes of the sky peeking through the branches and leaves.
The curl of a finger, the curve of a road.

If I don't paint, I forget to hear.
The call of a bird sitting on a post, the dog's nails clicking on
    the
wooden floor, the sigh of a friend after a sip of coffee.

If I don't paint, I forget how to filter my thoughts
and process my emotions. I forget how to love and how to rest.
I forget how to breathe. I forget the in and out, up and down,
ebb and flow rhythm of life itself.

To those that stifle the need to paint, to sing, make music, play,
dance, sculpt, write, act;
To those that don't create: Let this be your call,
stifle no more, you were made to create.
Please don't forget how to breathe.

—Heather Parker, *August 10, 2019*

56' fence painted by Heather and Megan Parker at Chautauqua Learn and Serve School. To see their stunning work, visit the school located on Magnolia Avenue. Image by Heather Parker

ANGELS

I know your face, but not your name.

I had exactly $49 to spend on groceries and household items.
Exactly $49. $8 over my limit at check-out,
I realized I miscounted.
As my toddler babbled in the cart, my very pregnant self,
ready to get home and into bed,
I asked the cashier to take a few items off.
You stepped over from behind me like an angel and said not to
worry, that you were going to pay for my entire bill.
It was at a time in my life when kindness was in short supply
and I had to keep myself from holding up the Walmart line,
dissolving into grateful tears. I met your eyes, kept my words to
"Thank you," and hoped you could see.

I know your face, but not your name.

My son got sick in the bathroom all over the floor.
He needed to be washed in the sink,
new clothes and underwear I didn't have on me.
I was struggling trying to clean up the mess,
keeping my daughter out of her brother's sick
and calming down an unwell child.
You stepped in and asked what size my son was in broken
English, coming back with new undies and an outfit.
While I changed him, you kept my daughter company.

I know your face, but not your name.

You saw me paying with change for two kids-meals, a rare treat
at the time. Sticking a $10 bill discreetly into my hand,
you said, "Merry Christmas."

I know your face, but not your name.

You stopped at my table on your way out the door and asked,
"Are you alright?"
I wasn't.

I know your face, but not your name.

You followed me for two miles because I had left my wallet on
top of the car and you wanted to be sure I didn't lose it.

I know your face, but not your name.

You made me feel safe and helped me change a tire on a dark
country road.

I know your face, but not your name.

You saw me struggling with groceries and two toddlers, so you
helped me to the door of my apartment.

And I hope you're all well.
I hope your life is full of the good stuff.
You helped my light not go out.
You reminded me that I'm not alone in this world.
Your kindness produced more of the same.
This corner of the world is brighter,
because you didn't look away.
I know you. I remember you.
My angels who haven't met a stranger.

—Sandi Klug Lard, *August 19, 2019*

WHAT I REMEMBER ARE THE SOUNDS

by Jan Prewett

What I remember are the sounds. October 10, 2018. The day broke with breeze—familiar and ordinary. With knowing what it heralded, however, there was a sense of foreboding. As the morning progressed, the winds began to build, and the sounds built with it.

There are basically three types of trees around where we live in Parker—oaks, pines, and palms. Each produces their own distinct sound. Pine needles brushing against each other make a whooshing whisper in a breeze while oaks are more guttural. Palms create a brittle rattle. Together, on a normal day, there is a harmony that scores the day. That Wednesday in October was not normal.

What began as a chorus became a discordant cacophony, and from there, something that defies description.

Sailboat tackle clanking against masts. The whining and then screaming of wind through power lines. The rat-tat-tat of leaves and twigs hitting structures and vehicles, becoming more like gunshots. The metal roofing slapping and then slamming as it relinquished its grip. The snapping and cracking of larger branches followed by thuds and bangs when they hit the ground or the house or the car.

Then the ever-increasing din became punctuated by the sound of my ears popping. That's when we took refuge in the closet under the stairs. I've heard people say it sounded like a freight train, but that's not right. It sounded like jet engine roar. Like fighter jets were parked in my front yard burning off excess fuel. And that's all I could hear. That's all I could hear.

Image by Jan Prewett

There are probably thousands of trees—many two, three feet in diameter—in my immediate vicinity. Most of those met their end while we were under the stairs, and yet I did not hear a single tree break or fall. Not one. All I heard was that roar.

Until the roof was ripped away. I heard that. Ripping, tearing, crashing, splitting, splintering. Deafening. Terrifying.

And then it began to recede. Not quickly, but steadily. The tempest became a storm, and that finally the storm became just wind, and then wind settled back into the breeze with which we'd begun the day—a day that was not normal.

What followed was silence. No cars. No air conditioners. Silence. And that was followed by a new cacophony which would last for weeks—generators and chain saws. The incessant beeping of trucks. Trucks repairing power lines—trucks picking up debris. More chainsaws, and then nail guns and saws as neighbors began to reassemble their lives.

Hurricane Michael. Wednesday, October 10, 2018. What I remember are the sounds—I hear them still.

Image by Jan Prewett

There are far better things ahead than any we leave behind.

— *C.S. LEWIS*

FAITH STANDS

As the winds roar,
As the waves rise higher,
As fear overcomes,
Faith stands.

As destruction grows,
As devastation overpowers,
As the broken cry out,
Faith stands.

As the world transforms,
As the road ahead darkens,
As we become weary,
Faith stands.

As we stumble forward,
As the shattering continues,
As our broken hearts grieve,
Faith stands.

As each new day dawns,
As seeds of hope spring forth,
As our determination strengthens,
Faith stands.

In the midst of the storm,
In the chaos of the aftermath,
In the struggle of rebuilding,
In the promise of tomorrow,
In the power of our healing,
Faith stands.

— Jennifer N. Fenwick, March 21, 2019

Image by Laura McManus

GET OVER IT

by Teri Elizabeth Hord

Like many of you, my husband and I recently watched the *Hurricane Man* documentary on the Science Channel. The episode was a two-hour special reliving what we all went though not quite one year ago.

One year.

That is still difficult for me to digest.

I watched my senior prom date in the fire station talk about how the walls were breathing and water was coming inside.

I watched the sweet fishing family go back to the marina after the storm to find that their boat, their entire life's work, had been completely destroyed.

I looked back at my engagement photos there and reminisced about when that boat had seen better days.

I watched the crew drive down the street that took me home every day for several years and marveled at all of the beautiful trees that are no longer there.

How quickly we do forget.

Places I used to not recognize after the storm, I now have a difficult time recognizing before.

I watched the girl dance in the front yard the day after Michael when she found out her boat was spared. She was embarrassed to "victory dance" on camera.

I did the same dance after realizing my home was not just a slab.

My heart aches for those who didn't.

I could feel what she felt.

Deep in my core, I could feel it all.

When the documentary was over, I made a choice.

It has almost been an entire year.

I need to move on.

I will move on.

The next night, we took our five-year-old to the temporary Halloween store on 23rd Street. He wants to be a pirate this year, amongst other things.

Walking in, I could feel it. That all too familiar feeling of loss. I found something to distract me.

We looked around the store, tried on wigs and masks, had a couple of scares and several laughs, but I needed to go to the restroom.

Where was it again? I'd been here 1,000 times.

I finally asked an employee and began to walk behind a black curtain, down the old game board aisle and back to the very back.

Toys-R-Us clearance stickers littered the dirty tile floor and several ceiling tiles were missing.

I wondered if water had come in. Was there mold?

"Stop."

We left the store and decided to have dinner at Outback. I was determined to keep my promise to myself.

"Get over this. It's fine."

There were several empty tables, but Outback, like everywhere else, is severely understaffed. We had a 20-minute wait, but after the remodel, there is nowhere to wait, so we went to sit outside.

Steve went inside to get us a drink while we waited. Camden and I sat and talked about how mommy used to work here, back when Outback was brand new, there was no Pier Park, and we would be on a 2 hour wait on the weekends.

"Where y'all from?" I heard a voice ask behind me.

I turned around to see an elderly gentleman and his wife sitting behind us. He had the same hat my Opa so proudly wears with the words "Vietnam Vet" displayed on the front.

"From here," I answered.

"On this side of the bridge or the other?"

"Oh, here we go," I thought. "I can't disrespect this man, but if I have to hear one more time how 'the beach had no damage,' I'm gonna scream!"

"On the other side. In Bay Point."

"Oh, I know it was really bad over there. My son lived there too."

"Yeah, it wasn't great, but we are really lucky. How 'bout y'all?"

"We live over in Springfield. Whew. That was a bad, bad storm. I'm glad we stayed though. She and I held the door shut for 3 and a half hours. Could a been worse. Can you believe it's been almost a year and it's still like this?"

"No, sir. I really can't."

Steve brought out the buzzing pager.

Our table was ready.

"Thank you so much for your service," I said.

And I stood up and walked away.

◆ ◆ ◆

Bad things do happen in the world, like war, natural disasters, disease. But out of those situations always arise stories of ordinary people doing extraordinary things.

— *DARYN KAGAN*

STRANGE NEW WORLD

by Jennifer N. Fenwick

It is like living in a strange new world. Landmarks the I used to pass by, often without a thought, are seen more clearly now in their absence.

The trees are bare, the ones still standing. Broken arms reaching toward the sky. Daily I see new specks of green emerging from their stark and gnarled branches. They stand a bit taller, like they're keeping vigil over the piles and piles of debris lining the streets.

Navigating once familiar roads, I often feel transported to a place far, far away from the one I knew. My heart hurts, but at the same time, I see life stretching to renew itself. Much like losing a loved one or a dear friend, the grief feels the same.

If I close my eyes I can see clearly the way things used to be. With eyes wide open though, the reminder that the landscape is so unquestionably different is ever present.

The people are the most changed. There's a certain look in the eyes now. We've survived what I imagine must feel like a war. The enemy came, blowing through our existence and forever altering us. Much like the barren landscape, there's an emptiness in the eyes. A sadness that says, yes, I'm still here, but everything is so different now.

I remember feeling that way when I lost my father and my best friend. The world around me went on, but I was stuck somewhere between that last moment, that last breath, and the strange new world I now faced without them. I think we're all grieving in that way. Grieving, but hopeful too, that we'll be able to laugh again, breathe again, and feel joy again in this strange new world.

When Hurricane Michael slammed into our cities, he took more with him than just our trees, our businesses, our homes. He took pieces of us. Memories we'd planted long ages. I was happy to discover, recently, that one of those pieces is now back where it belongs. Loving placed two year ago in memory of my dear friend and compassionate member of our community by those who understood her love of books, Alisa's Library is back in place in our walking park where it belongs. Though the trees and boardwalk are gone, her spirit remains. Image by Sharon Owens.

WHAT I LEARNED IN THE AFTERMATH OF A MAJOR STORM

by Tracy Johnstone

What I learned about what you really need those first few weeks after a major hurricane devastates your community.

Go buy a few burner phones from the opposite carrier from what you have. Do this now. Hedge your bet on which one if any will work. The kind of satellite phone most of us can afford does not work.

Get multiple AM/FM radios and batteries—they will likely be the only news or information source you will have for quite some time.

Fill up cars AND a dozen gas cans—No power no gas. In our case pumps destroyed, so no gas—literally. No internet when power is back; no credit cards anywhere. No cash, no gas.

Get cash now. When the banks were closed for three weeks cash was hard to come by. If you are a business owner get enough cash to make a one-week payroll at least. No internet so no payroll processing. The auto deposit or pay card would be useless to your employees anyway.

Communicate with your payroll company and make plans for after the storm. Loop in your CPA.

If you are in the cone, assume the worst. Contact friends and family who live elsewhere as they will be your lifeline to the real world. Zello or Facebook Messenger may be the only way to communicate with them.

Honestly, filing a claim will be the least of your worries those first few weeks—you cannot do it anyway with no phones, power, or internet.

Make a connection plan with employees and family— "We will meet at this location to help each other and connect as soon as we can after the storm." When you go there, and no one is there—leave a message posted about your status and when you will be back. Eventually you will connect. During this time when you want to tell someone something you have to drive to them to tell them.

To buy, or not to buy?

Do not buy just small bottle waters—if it is a direct hit you will have more bottle water pouring into your town than anyone could drink. But, you do need large volumes of water for flushing toilets, washing dishes, bathing. So fill the bathtubs, get a clean trash can you can sit outside to collect rainwater, get those large camping plastic water containers out if you have them—and fill them.

That will be your water crisis.

Get some chlorine tablets or bleach to sanitize your water.

Sanitation will quickly become one of the biggest issues in your community. No running water, flushing toilets, hot water for hand wash, working outside in the nasty conditions, everything inside feels yuck with no AC or power, food spoilage, etc. Staying well becomes something you actually have to work for. A camping toilet seat and bucket was our bathroom at our office for about two weeks. Pick one up.

Buy a large solar shower bag—sit it in the sun to warm. By day five you will thank me. Buy baby wipes and cheap thin wash clothes. You will be stinky beyond belief if it is 90 degrees and 80% humidity for weeks afterwards.

Stock up on paper plates, forks, napkins etc.—washing dishes with no running water is not fun. Get two old fashion dish pans to do the dishes—you can't fill up a sink with water. One for washing one for rinsing in that bleach water.

Buy the generator—as big as you can afford. Test it out and have it ready before the storm. If you can get a whole house generator it will change your life post-storm and your neighbors. By the way they need oil, or they will shut down.

Get several propane bottles if you have a gas grill or lots of bags of charcoal. It will be the best tasting meat ever as you try to cook up what is thawing in the refrigerator.

You need a day kit. Have sunscreen and bug spray and body wipes in your day kit. Take everything you might need for the day when you head out. *Everything.* Advil, food, drinks, change of clothes. You don't have the gas, energy, or time to make unnecessary trips.

Speaking of trips—what took 15-20 minutes to drive to before the storm will take hours after. For me it was almost three hours for that short trip a dozen times or more. It will make you crazy, defeated, and overwhelmed but it will get better.

Food—bread, peanut butter, jelly—knife and spoon. I cannot tell you how many people I made a PBJ for out of the back of my car for weeks. Buy some bread and freeze it. Keep paper towels, those skinny wash clothes, etc. —handing someone a washcloth you have soaked in the cooler in the ice is a gift from above.

I lost 8 pounds in the first two weeks after the storm. You will forget to eat. You will sweat off the pounds. You WILL get dehydrated if you don't pay attention. Between the heat, doing physical labor 8 or more hours a day outside, the stress—we were all on the hurricane recovery diet.

Fill every cooler with ice and keep them inside not in the hot garage. You just won't believe how big a deal having ice will become. If you own a restaurant go get all the ice from the ice makers you can before it melts. Have folks bag some up and put in a working freezer as backup.

Curfews—make the very most out of the curfew hours you have if you need to get out to see about a business or others. It already gets dark earlier and you have to be home by sunset.

If you have a weapon know where it is, check it, and carry if you have a permit. Looting is a very scary thing to watch happen and very scary when it happens in your own neighborhood.

Do not talk publicly about what you have at your home. People truly become desperate so keep the fact you have a generator, food, ice, large volumes of water, gas, etc.—to yourself and only share if you intend to share.

Do gather your important papers and photos, etc.—when your ceiling falls in and everything is wet, the wind is 155 mph, and you are scared, you will not be in a state of mind to start looking and it is probably too late at that point.

Mold starts to grow in just a few days with no power/AC with everything wet. The papers inside of a drawer will be moldy.

If it is bad like Michael there will be no mail running for weeks, no FedEx/UPS delivering, no banking, no internet, no phone service cell or land line. No medical services if hospitals are destroyed like ours were—we had a 100% evacuation of every patient and nursing home patient from our area following the storm.

When they say get your medicine it is real. With no power, internet, deliveries for weeks, there is nowhere to fill a script and no delivery to have someone send it to you.

People who lose everything and people who have damage are two VERY different storm survivors.

Buy the best chain saw you can—forget trash bags and rakes we are talking trees here.

The tree trimmers show up first, the tarpers, then the debris moving people, the abatement/interior demo people (the most dangerous bunch). Then the roofers, the window people, the random contractors, more debris removal people. The signs go up for flooring, sheetrock, painting, cabinets. You can watch the progression of things by who's real-estate sign was planted at the entrance to your community the night before.

Buy tarps, furring strips to nail it to the roof, roofing nails, a ladder that reaches your roof. The longer you wait to tarp the faster the mold will come—and it will come.

You will not have garbage pickup for many weeks—have some outside trash bags to store the garbage in so it is not so nasty.

If you get a newspaper delivered, the first day it shows up after the storm will be a huge sign of hope for things getting better.

Take lots of pictures—and I mean lots. Take pre-storm pictures of your home, inside your refrigerator, pantry, cabinets. Take post-storm pictures, but not just with insurance in mind. Just take them of *everything* that you are shocked about—which will be *everything*. You will be glad you did.

If you can reach someone out of town that has power, internet, and phone, they can call in your claim to insurance and FEMA for you. So get someone your policy info if you can. It just gets you in the very long que but nothing much happens with insurance for quite some time.

Possibly you, and if not many other someone's will need temp shelter/housing. The shelters will already be full. If you work for a large company like Publix they will bring in temporary shelters such as bunk-house-like trailers, shower/bathroom trailers, trailers that have washers and dryers running off generators and portable water tanks, etc.—And an ice truck which is amazing and free to everyone.

You will always remember the traffic, the five or more hours a day in your car. The heat and humidity, how quiet everything is, the smoke and security alarms going off for days on end all day and all night—that will really be all you hear at first. You will hear the helicopters doing search and rescue. Next, the chain saws—and that goes on for months.

You will be in shock. You just will. It is numbing to see so much destruction. You will not remember details about the days after the storm. I wish I had journaled or taken notes every day—just a little something to help me look back and process what happened.

You will appreciate and understand who "your people are" because they will show up in force. The five-star ones will show up without being asked. You will need those you love and care about to bear witness to what happened. You just need to be seen.

Many will not get it. If you are alive then you are okay to them. You desperately need physical help, desperately. But you need the support. You will be in a grieving period shortly afterwards. Shock and trauma coupled with pure raw physical exertion is debilitating. If you own a business you can multiply all of that by a 100.

People will not grasp the gravity of what has happened and frankly it would hard for anyone to. They will never know how much you needed them when they did not come—a conversation I had with dozens of folks. Just let it go and appreciate those who are there. You will be surprised who comes to your aid and those who just truck on as if nothing has happened. And you will *still* be okay.

Our community is in no way able to handle another hurricane—physically much less mentally.

It's not just the actual time the hurricane makes landfall but when you have lived this you know what it means for the next few years of your life after it has passed over. When the big one hits you will be traumatized by the experience *and* the aftermath.

You will *never* be the same.

◆ ◆ ◆

WRECKED

What have we got?
We've got

Less builders than building
More rubble than rooves

We've got

Front yard camping
People living in cars

Forests that are kindling
Time bombs of flaming fear

We've got

More patients than patience
Less doctors than docks

Condoms on our chimneys
Cause we're still getting screwed

We've got

Elephants blaming Asses
Donkeys blaming Derms

Grandstanding politicians
Walking like cocks

The only shade we're getting is from
Those elected to serve

We've got each other
But more leave every day
Now a new season is here
What do you say?

— *Jason Hedden, June 1, 2019*

Image by Jason Hedden

MISTY EDGES

The misty edges of this watered-down landscape,

altered beyond imagining.

Floating remnants

of disjointed memories,

lost swiftly to this happenstance.

Sweeping greyscale overshadowing

Colors once painted in hues

of boldest greens and deepest reds,

and the most vivid splatters of blue.

In this murky dwelling we plod along

breathing air with our battered lungs.

We broken poets with bleeding pens,

forming words with our silent tongues.

And the white gulls cry as the boats set sail

to disappear within the mist.

Their pleading songs skim across the bay,

when did our lives transform to this?

In this long farewell, standing on the shore,

as the masts retire from view,

so too our souls turn a weary eye,

from the world that we once knew.

— *Jennifer N. Fenwick, June 28, 2019*

Photo by John Fenwick

BEAUTY IN THE BROKEN

by Teri Elizabeth Hord

May 22, 2019—Shell Island has been a sanctuary of sorts for me since the storm. There is something soothing about the warm sun on my face, the sound of the crashing waves, and the salt air that helps ease some of the pain.

For a few hours at least, the blue tarps, rumblings of tractors, and seemingly endless to-do lists disappear and are replaced with immense beauty and tranquility. I would go there every day if I could.

During our last trip, Camden and I looked for shells, or "treasures" as we call them.

He proudly held up one of his newfound treasures. "Look at this one, Mommy!"

"Oh, yeah. Look at that. That's too bad. That one would've been so pretty if it wasn't broken."

He looked at me puzzled.

"Well, I love it! I don't care if it's broken. I'm keeping it!"

Beauty through the eyes of a child.

I felt ashamed for a moment.

Who am I to tell him what's beautiful?

And he was right. It was a very nice treasure.

In that moment, my 5-year-old unknowingly taught me an incredible life lesson, as he so often does. In so many ways, we can all relate. Those of us that are still here have, one way or another, chosen to be here. Our community is broken, yes, but we choose to wake up every single day and continue to move forward the best we know how.

Photo by Teri Elizabeth Hord

So many have posted pictures of sunflowers growing in random places or breathtaking sunsets through broken trees.

You've found the beauty in the broken.

The same lesson applies to us as people.

There have been times since the storm I have surprised myself with my strength and resiliency to navigate through all of this unchartered territory.

Unfortunately, there have also been times I've surprised myself at how poorly I've handled certain situations, letting my emotions and my anger get the best of me.

I guess I'm broken, too.

Thankfully, I am able to surround myself with people that love me anyway.

People that see past my flaws.

People that still think I'm beautiful inside and out, even when I do lose it!

So far, month seven has been a great month for us here in Panama City. HomeGoods, TJ Maxx, 5 Guys, Zaxby's, and That's Too Cute have all reopened.

President Trump officially approved the federal government's 90-percent cost share for public assistance. *Thank you, sir.*

They finally started tearing down the Grocery Outlet on 15th and Beck Avenue.

And my personal favorite, the remaining trees have finally blossomed and there is the greenest vegetation visible here since October 9,2018.

So today, I'm choosing to see the beauty in the broken.

The good over the bad.

The strength over the weakness.

The kindness over the bitterness.

We are all broken in some ways, but we are all beautiful in so many others.

Don't toss out all the broken shells.

Keep going and looking for the beauty.

◆ ◆ ◆

In the center of a hurricane there is absolute peace and quiet.

There is no safer place than in the center of the will of God.

— *CORRIE TEN BOOM*

NEW FENCE

Our fence is new.
Our roof repaired.
But our children lost their home.
We have our faith.
Hold on to hope.
Though the road ahead is long.
Our trees are sprouting green again.
The few that did survive.
We have returned to living.
Though we didn't choose this life.
Our hearts beat a little faster,
When thunder clouds roll in.
We find it hard to breathe now,
With the rising of the wind.
We understand the heartache,
of the ones who've faced this storm.
In the Bayou, on the Islands,
On the Coasts and on the Shores.
We aren't victims of a punishment.
Or unlucky in the least.
We're simply just survivors,
standing firm on battered feet.
There is no rhyme or reason.
No deeper meaning to discern.
Mother Nature chose her path,
and once chosen didn't turn.

Our fence is new.
Our roof repaired.
But that's the easy part.
Much harder now to overcome,
This grief deep in our hearts.

—Jennifer N. Fenwick, November 24, 2018

NEVER PREPARED

by Teri Elizabeth Hord

June first. Most people think of June as the beginning of summer. The official kick-off to sunshine, longer days, and relaxation.

The kids are out of school.

The weather is warm.

Beach days, pool parties, and BBQ's are in our near future.

But, here, this year, it's different.

Sure, we're excited about summer, too, but we also know in the back of our minds, today marks the beginning of hurricane season. The dreaded day we've all known was coming is finally upon us.

Hurricane preparedness is all the rage today. I watched it on Good Morning America and the Today Show. Jim Cantore is in Mexico Beach urging folks to prepare and showing them what a hurricane is really capable of. Better get those battery-operated flashlights ready! Don't forget the canned goods!

How do you prepare to be without cell service or power or water for days, maybe weeks, after the storm finally passes?

How do you prepare to find an affordable rental because your home is unlivable, but now the rent has skyrocketed to three times what is was yesterday and you just lost your job?

How do you prepare to lose everything?

You don't.

Most of us are through the initial shock. We are all working our way through the grief. We all have different ways of coping and are

186

Photo by Teri Elizabeth Hord

healing at different paces. It's been almost 8 months, but we are far from recovered.

How do you prepare for PTSD, survivor's guilt, and just grief in general?

How do you prepare for something you're still reeling from?

You can't.

So, today, we make sure we have plenty of water, non-perishable foods, flashlights, and batteries. We take all the precautions and do all the things.

But in the backs of our minds, we all know we can never truly be prepared, and we're all terrified.

"Prepare," they say.

But how?

How do you prepare to end up with your children in a bathtub or under a mattress begging, pleading for the wind to stop?

I think I can fit a couple more cases of water next to my grandmother's ceramic Christmas tree. And next time, I will be filling my bathtub with water. I can say from experience, filling five-gallon buckets with dirty canal water in 90-degree heat at low tide was not my favorite activity.

But, I guess I should have been more prepared.

Life is a hurricane, and we board up to save what we can and bow low to the earth to crouch in that small space above the dirt where the wind will not reach. We honor anniversaries of deaths by cleaning graves and sitting next to them before fires, sharing food with those who will not eat again. We raise children and tell them other things about who they can be and what they are worth—to us, everything. We love each other fiercely, while we live and after we die.

We survive.

— **JESMYN WARD**

WELCOME STUDENTS

A new school year begins,
in this strange new world.
Teachers open their classrooms,
welcoming students.
The homeless ones.
The ones whose friends
have moved away.
The determined ones.
The day dawns bright and clear.
With renewed hope.
Eager minds crossing the thresholds.
With ready smiles.
With abundant faith.
This year will be the best one yet.
Despite the losses.
Despite the storm.
Recovery has never looked more promising.
Hope has never seemed more real.

—Jennifer N. Fenwick, August 12, 2019

Photo courtesy of Pixabay

WE ARE NOT OK

by Jennifer N. Fenwick

February 27, 2019—My dear friend, Linda Artman, shared a story with me that made me sad. She was flying into Panama City to spend a few weeks volunteering in the area, as she has done many times since Hurricane Michael, and to assist me with book promotions for *In the Eye of the Storm*, of which she is a contributing author.

She had a conversation with one of the airline hostesses, the topic of which, after further reflection, I consider to be at the heart of the current lack of understanding and support we are currently receiving outside the Panhandle.

When asked what her destination was, Linda replied, "I'm headed to Panama City to spend a few weeks helping out with recovery."

To which the hostess replied, "Oh, it's not so bad there."

Linda was taken aback. So she asked the hostess, " Have you been to Panama City or any of the other impacted areas?"

"Oh yes," the woman replied, "I've flown into airport many times."

Linda probed further, "Have you gone over the bridge into town?"

"No," the woman responded, "But it's all the same area, really."

At this point Linda was getting increasingly frustrated with the conversation and the woman. "I can assure you," Linda explained to the woman, "The areas west of the bridge, Panama City, Lynn Haven, Springfield, Callaway, and most definitely Mexico Beach, are NOT ok.

The devastation in those areas, and even in areas north of there, is widespread and catastrophic."

The woman just shrugged. Linda knew she wasn't making any impact on her at all. So she offered, "I'd be glad to take you and some of your colleagues with me so you can see firsthand what the residents are dealing with."

The woman shook her head, "No that's ok," she replied, "I'm good."

"That's the problem," Linda conveyed to me sadly, "People just don't know, and they don't care enough to see for themselves; to correct their misperceptions."

"That's human nature, though isn't it," I replied, " It's much easier to keep your blinders on and to perpetuate the half-truths than it is to actually look into it yourself. If you do that, then you have to take responsibility."

If you come into the Panhandle and your only destination is the beach, then yes, you will definitely leave with the misguided thought that everything is ok, normal even. However, I can assure you, as can the thousands of residents who are living in the aftermath of Michael, we are not ok! The impacted areas ARE NOT OK!

Damage to Mexico Beach has been compared to that of Katrina in southern Mississippi in 2005, where entire communities were flattened by wind and storm surge. Panama City and its surrounding municipalities will take years to rebuild.

We are facing a housing crisis with many people homeless with nowhere to go. There are currently almost 5,000 displaced and homeless in Bay County alone, including many school-aged children, since the storm. That's an increase of over 500%!

Heavy damage and complete destruction to many multi-family and fixed-income apartment complexes have compounded the problem. Currently, Rising insurance claims have pushed property losses in the affected areas over $4.8 billion.

Many businesses are closed long-term due to heavy damage. Many others are not reopening at all.

Downed trees still decorate most every street and neighborhood in the region, along with the ever-present blue tarps and roofing collateral from those fortunate enough to actually be getting a new roof.
Photo by Felix Mizioznikov/Shutterstock

Bay District Schools (BDS) has suffered a student population drop of almost 5,000 students since Michael. The District is also experiencing the loss of teachers, support staff, and administrators. If the downward trend continues, major reductions in teaching staff could become a problem for the District. To put it into perspective, 5,000 fewer students, an 18% reduction, equals 637 jobs.

The reduction in ad valorem taxes due to a widespread reduction in taxable values, as well as the decreased student population, has put the current financial loss to the District due to Michael in excess of $300 million.

State officials estimate that Hurricane Michael created about 20 million cubic tons of debris from Mexico Beach into Georgia as he barreled through the region on October 10, 2018. Hurricane Irma, which cut a path from the Florida Keys to Jacksonville in 2017, resulted in about 2 million cubic tons of debris by comparison.

Though massive debris piles from the storm have lessened considerably, the abundance of rebuilding and constant construction has created new piles in their place.

Progress is being made. However, the scarred landscape and bare, broken trees will take years to rehabilitate and flourish.

Health officials report that increased signs of mental health problems and trauma are common following major disasters like Michael. Experiencing a disaster of this magnitude is a stressful event and anxiety and depression are common in the aftermath.

Research into post-storm and other major disasters show that between 30 and 40 percent of victims develop Post-Traumatic Stress Disorder (PTSD). It has been shown that following major events like, Katrina, Harvey, Florence, and now Michael, that PTSD can affect how people function in their jobs and personal relationships, as well as how quickly the community as a whole recovers.

"We've survived a major catastrophic event, yes, but everything we knew is gone."

To those who perpetuate the myth that Hurricane Michael "wasn't that bad;" That, "aside from a few downed trees and damaged structures everything is normal;" That, "almost six months later everything is ok;" I implore you, come see for yourself. Come visit these areas. Walk around with your eyes wide-open. Talk with the residents, the survivors, the ones living daily in the aftermath. Volunteer to assist those aiding with the ongoing relief and rebuilding efforts. Do ANYTHING, but continue to propagate the misinformation and false perceptions.

I guarantee you that not one of us who've lived through Michael, what he took and what he left behind, will tell you we're ok.

We're hopeful. We're determined. We're anxious and hurting. We're scarred. We're changed. We're steadfast. We're healing. On any given day we're one or all of this. But since October 10, we have not been, nor are we now ok.

◆ ◆ ◆

And once the storm is over, you won't remember how you made it through, how you managed to survive. You won't even be sure, whether the storm is really over. But one thing is certain. When you come out of the storm, you won't be the same person who walked in. That's what the storm is all about.

— **HARUKI MURAKAMI**

IN THIS NEW WORLD

In this new world.

we are shattered, hopeful souls.

Bearing losses of unimaginable depth.

Shouldering the burden of

staggering, debilitating grief.

In this new world,

we are determined warriors.

Maintaining our faith in the face

of insurmountable odds.

Believing still, that even alone,

we will rise again.

In this new world, we press onward.

Without another choice,

how can we do less?

In this new world, we are the broken,

the huddled masses.

Praying for healing.

Seeing past the destruction,

past the crippling fear,

to the promise present in every dawn.

That this too shall pass.

That we'll emerge.

That we will rise from these ashes,

changed but steadfast.

Bruised but willing.

Scarred but magnificent,

in our conviction

that our greatest asset,

is and has always been

our hopeful, willing, unbreakable spirit.

—*Jennifer N. Fenwick, May 13, 2019*

MEET A FEW OF OUR CONTRIBUTORS

Linda Artman enjoys hearing people's stories and then sharing them in meaningful ways to help others understand and care about specific events or experiences. She brings a deep concern for people, fueled by her own experiences and her compassion for helping others, to the way she tells their stories.

As an Air Force wife for twenty years Linda, her husband, Dave, and their two sons had the opportunity to live in several states and Europe. These experiences enriched their lives and broadened their perspectives. For twelve years Linda was a teacher of students from kindergarten to adults. She was a flight attendant for twenty years, flying on that horrific 9/11, which deepened her resolve to speak up about the contributions of flight crews when people discuss the events of that day.

She has spent her retirement joyfully caring for grandchildren whenever possible, volunteering as part of Bay County's recovery in many capacities post Hurricane Michael and at the Flight 93 Memorial in Shanksville, Pennsylvania.

Photo courtesy of Tasha Shelley of Shelly Photography.

Hurricane Michael was not **Melinda JD Hall's** first nor last storm. Migrating here from Louisiana, Hurricane Katrina was her family's first major storm.

Melinda is the mother of 4 and has had the privilege of loving her late husband, Sean, for 25 years. He passed from Angiosarcoma the day after Christmas following Michael. "Each storm has prepared us for the next."

Melinda started her career as an RN and is now retired, she uses her talent to nurse through verse. She became a published author and illustrator publishing her first children's book, *A Seed of Change*, available through Dorrance Publishing and Amazon and is under contract for her second publication, *Mother Earth*.

Melinda has many exciting projects in the works. An artist, you can find her beautiful works available at *Gypsy Beach Treasured Kreations* in St. Andrew's Panama City and online under her own company name, *Uriel's Uniquities, LLC* via Instagram, Etsy, and Facebook.

"Our storms are never over. They may have different context, different damage, and different names, but we will always lower our sails, point out bow toward the headwinds, and ride out stronger than before."

Jason Hedden is a teacher, actor and director. He is currently a Professor of Theatre and Chair of Visual & Performing Arts at Gulf Coast State College in Panama City, FL. He is a frequent public speaker on the topics of arts and education and has recently been working as a writer and stand-up comedian. He enjoys traveling and spending time exploring the outdoors with his wife and son. Visit Jason online at www.jasonhedden.com.

Kim Hill is a freelance writer, author, painter, award-winning photographer, and overall Jill-of-All-Trades who lives in Florida. Kim has two degrees in Criminology and is also an advocate for SkinCancer.net.

Kim recently had three of her photographs selected for the Clio Art Fair in Chelsea, NYC and was just offered a book deal for her photojournalism on abandoned areas along Northwest Florida and another book deal on abandoned places following Hurricane Michael.

Teri Hord is a wife, mother, and lifelong resident of Bay County.

After graduating from Florida State University in 2010, she moved back to Panama City where she met her husband, Steve, also a Bay County native. They own and operate a local home inspection business and have two sons.

While writing has always been a passion of hers, in the months following the storm, it became a vital outlet in order to foster strength and healing. Visit Teri's blog at https://survivingthestorm101018.wordpress.com/.

❖   ❖   ❖

ABOUT THE AUTHOR

Jennifer N. Fenwick was born and raised in Panama City, FL. After marrying her husband, John, they moved to Phoenix, AZ where John was born, Three years later, they moved back to the Florida Panhandle to be closer to Jennifer's family and the members of John's family who now resided there. Their daughter, Nichole, now 29, was just one when they returned to Panama City. Their daughter, Emma, now 20, was born and raised in Panama City.

Jennifer is a former Bay County teacher who now works professionally as a program analyst and technical editor for a government contractor. Her first book, *Four Weeks: A Journey from Darkness* was released on Amazon on October 6, just four days before Hurricane Michael hit the Gulf Coast.

Jennifer is both a contributor and the editor for *In the Eye of the Storm* and *In the Aftermath of the Storm*. Both books are the result of the generous submissions and contributions of stories, poetry, artwork, and photography from survivors of Hurricane Michael in Bay in surrounding counties.

For Jennifer, this experience has been a true labor of love, and a healing balm in the face of so much destruction.

◆ ◆ ◆

All royalties earned from the sale of this book go to the United Way of Northwest Florida's Hurricane Michael Relief Fund. 100% of all Hurricane Michael donations will be applied to LOCAL relief efforts in the Northwest Florida area.

For donations visit http://unitedwaynwfl.org/

209

Made in the USA
Coppell, TX
26 October 2019